D0923938

CAPITAL AND TIME

CURRENCIES

New Thinking for Financial Times

Melinda Cooper and Martijn Konings, Series Editors

Capital and Time

For a New Critique of Neoliberal Reason

MARTIJN KONINGS

Stanford University Press
Stanford, California

Stanford University Press
Stanford, California

© 2018 by the Board of Trustees of the Leland Stanford Junior University.
All rights reserved.

No part of this book may be reproduced or transmitted in any form or by any means, electronic or mechanical, including photocopying and recording, or in any information storage or retrieval system without the prior written permission of Stanford University Press.

Printed in the United States of America on acid-free, archival-quality paper

Library of Congress Cataloging-in-Publication Data

Names: Konings, Martijn, 1975– author.
Title: Capital and time : for a new critique of neoliberal reason / Martijn Konings.
Other titles: Currencies (Series)
Description: Stanford, California : Stanford University Press, 2018. | Series: Currencies: new thinking for financial times | Includes bibliographical references and index.
Identifiers: LCCN 2017019565| ISBN 9781503603905 (cloth : alk. paper) | ISBN 9781503604438 (pbk. : alk. paper) | ISBN 9781503604445 (e-book)
Subjects: LCSH: Speculation. | Capital market. | Finance—Government policy. | Capitalism. | Neoliberalism.
Classification: LCC HG6015 .K66 2018 | DDC 332/.041—dc23
LC record available at https://lccn.loc.gov/2017019565

Typeset by Classic Typography in 10/15 Janson

Contents

CAPITAL AND TIME

INTRODUCTION

Beyond the Critique of Speculation

The most real thing is money, but money is nothing more than a form of debt,
which is to say a commitment to pay money at some time in the future.
The whole system is therefore fundamentally circular and self-referential.
There is nothing underneath, as it were, holding it up.
—Mehrling 1999: 138.

Following the financial crisis of 2007–8, many progressive academics and commentators loudly declared that the event was simply the manifestation of what they had long argued—namely, that rampant speculation in unregulated financial markets was fuelling an unstable accumulation of financial claims entirely out of balance with fundamental values, and that this would sooner or later lead to a massive crisis (see, among many others, Baker 2009; Wray 2009; Gamble 2009; Cohan 2010; Stiglitz 2010; Foster and Magdoff 2009). As financial structures threatened to deleverage, progressive intelligentsia rushed to ring the death knell for the neoliberal policies of deregulation and nonintervention that they viewed as having given free rein to the market's "animal spirits," Keynes's term for the speculative impulses of the financial sector. At the height of the crisis, in the second half of 2008, as the American government moved to prop up some of the country's major financial institutions, excitement about the "return of the state" was palpable. The morally problematic aspects of the bailouts did not go unnoticed, of course, but those were seen as only underscoring the basic lesson of the episode—that the financial system is unable to regulate itself and requires external interventions for there to be a coherent economic order. The future, it was argued, belonged to public regulation and Keynesian steering.

This has turned out to be a serious misreading of the crisis. Instead of a "new New Deal" (Krugman 2009: xix), we got a neoliberalism recharged. Far from a political turning point, the crisis has been the occasion for an entrenchment of neoliberal principles and an extension of its operative mechanisms (Mirowski 2013; Cahill 2014; Dardot and Laval 2014). The financial sector has not only restored most of its precrisis sources of profit, but it has also opened up a range of new opportunities for speculative investment, not least in areas that feed directly off the significant insecurity and dislocation wrought by the crisis itself (Soederberg 2014). And yet, awareness that initial assessments were mistaken has prompted only limited efforts to rethink the critique of neoliberal capitalism. All too often, the unexpected resilience of neoliberalism is only taken as so much more evidence of the fundamental irrationality of faith in the self-regulating properties of the market. At the same time as capital unearths new sources of value to validate its speculations, the critics of neoliberal capitalism are back to announcing the unsustainable nature of financial speculation and the inevitable arrival of the next—this time truly final—crisis of neoliberal capitalism (Duncan 2012; Hudson 2012; Crouch 2011; Lapavitsas 2014; Streeck 2014; Kotz 2015; Keen 2017; Durand 2017).

The critique of speculation as an irresponsible bet on the future, one unwarranted by fundamental values, has always been an important element of the heterodox critique of capitalism, but it has become its centerpiece during the neoliberal era—which, it is certainly true, has given a huge boost to the speculative dimension of capitalism. Where mainstream economic theory often discerns little more than self-correcting deviations from an equilibrium state, critical and heterodox perspectives find irrational forces that are responsible for the periodic build-up of unsustainable, top-heavy structures of fictitious claims. That dynamic, they argue, must sooner or later come to a halt when foundational values reassert themselves and overleveraged financial structures begin to unravel. Such reasoning has become closely associated with a cyclical theory of capitalist development that views speculation as a sort of congenital pathology—a problem that rears its head with a certain regularity and corrupts some of the system's normal functions. This way of thinking is epitomized and formalized in the contemporary return to the work of Karl Polanyi (1944), whose concept of the "double movement" posits that history evolves in cycles: periodic "disembedding" movements, when the speculative logic of the market becomes unmoored from its social foundations, are inevitably followed by "re-embedding" movements, when the state intervenes to resubordinate markets by reimposing limits and restoring foundations (Blyth 2002; Abdelal 2009; Dale 2010; Streeck 2012; Fraser 2013; Block and Somers 2014).

The critique of speculation harkens back to an older critique of money and finance: the critique of chrematistics in antiquity, as well as the way the latter was reformulated as a critique of the idolatrous worship of money in premodern Christianity. In this tradition, speculation is depicted as an investment in promises that lack foundation, as the irrational attribution of value to fictions devoid of substance. At the heart of the heterodox critique of contemporary capitalism, then, is a distinction between real and fictitious value; speculation is seen to generate financial forms that lack substance and whose claim to value is fake or illusory. That the orthodoxy of the past is today's heterodoxy is an almost too obvious clue as to the conservative and anachronistic character of the critique of speculation. The modern subject speculates not in defiance of fundamental values but precisely because secular life offers no such foundations to fall back on. At an experiential level, moderns readily intuit that not speculating is not an option, and that their speculations are pragmatically motivated positions in an interactive dynamic of speculation, that is, in a logic of specularity (Orléan 1989; Vogl 2015: 113). Value has no existence apart from the pragmatics of valuation, which are always anticipatory, bound up with expectations of the use that new connections are likely to have for us (Muniesa 2011). We are forever faced with the practical impossibility of distinguishing between a position that is speculative and one that is oriented to real values (Esposito 2011: 77).

This book argues that the critique of speculation as it has been widely adopted in such critical fields as political economy, economic sociology, and heterodox economics, as well as in progressively minded public commentary on the state of economic life, represents a conceptual and political dead end. Not only is it misleading as a general approach; it is also incapable of recognizing how the neoliberal reconstruction of American capitalism has actively engaged this speculative dimension and the specific ordering mechanisms and governance rationalities it has thereby engendered. This chapter introduces three themes that the rest of the book will elaborate more systematically: the speculative nature of economic value; the role of banking as a normalizing dynamic within the logic of risk; and the significance of neoliberalism in reconfiguring the place of speculation, risk, and banking in governance.

Plastic Value

When one considers that the critique of foundationalism (in the form of various anti-essentialist, postmodern, and postpositivist turns) has had a tremendous impact on almost every branch of the social sciences with any critical ambitions, there is something truly odd about the fact that the routine appeal to ontological value foundations made by the critique of speculation enjoys the degree of legitimacy that it does. The situation becomes even more puzzling given that the critique of foundationalism has hardly bypassed fields such as political economy and economic sociology. Indeed, the critique of economic determinism and essentialism—or "economism"—is one of their main conceptual pillars, and the idea that economic actors and institutions are socially, culturally, or otherwise "constructed" has profoundly shaped the development of these fields.

We might say that heterodox perspectives tend to understand the relation between real and fictitious value as "elastic": the material of value can be stretched or inflated through speculation, but at a certain point it will either have to be allowed to return to its original state—or it will snap. The difficulty here has been the inability to specify, with even a minimal degree of accuracy, the parameters that govern value's stretchability. Modern capitalism enjoys a strong track record of disproving progressive predictions of financial collapse (Konings 2011). Throughout the twentieth century, predictions of the critical breaking point have been revised upward in response to capitalism's ability to sustain higher levels of speculative activity. Indeed, from a certain historical vantage point, one that commands a bird's-eye view of centuries of financial history, what stands out is perhaps not so much how speculative activity erodes order, but rather that the rise of speculative finance has also seen the emergence of powerful ordering institutions, such as a stable monetary unit and central banks, which enjoy a definite (if never unconditional) ability to regulate the value of the currency.

Calder's overview of a half century of predictions of financial collapse triggered by growing consumer debt illustrates the point here.

Fifty years of headlines in the periodical press show that consumer credit has never lacked for nervous critics:

Harper's, 1940 (when consumer indebtedness was $5.5 billion): "Debt Threatens Democracy"

Business Week, 1949 (when consumer indebtedness had doubled to $11.6 billion): "Is the Country Swamped with Debt?"

U.S. News & World Report, 1959 (when consumer debt had tripled again to $39.2 billion): "Never Have So Many Owed So Much"

Nation, 1973 (when consumer debt had quadrupled again to $155.1 billion): "Mountain of Debt"

Changing Times, 1989 (when consumer debt had increased another fivefold to $795 billion): "Are We over Our Heads in Debt?"

U.S. News & World Report, 1997 (when debt stood at $1.2 trillion): "In
   Debt All the Way up to Their Nose Rings (Generation X)"

After examining a half century of such articles, the historian who reads
in his newspaper "Credit-Card Debt Could Be the Plastic Explosive
That Blasts the Economy in '97" can be forgiven for calmly turning to
the sports page. (Calder 1999: 292–93)

For the sake of completeness, we should add that consumer debt in
2007 stood at $2.5 trillion, and by the end of 2016 it had grown to $3.8
trillion (Board of Governors of the Federal Reserve System 2017).

From the point of view of orthodox economic theory, all this would
simply serve to underscore the futility of second-guessing market prices,
the forms in which values appear and are communicated. Although that
is not the argument this book will make, the difficulty of translating the
heterodox critique of speculation into practically insightful terms does
suggest the need to revisit orthodox understandings of value and money,
and to consider how the latter might register or express something that
the heterodox critique has been unable to acknowledge or thematize.
My claim in this respect is that in its eagerness to reject the orthodox
understanding of money as incorrect, heterodox theory has generally
been blind to the work done by that conception, how it articulates and
adds force to the regulative imaginaries and affective structuration of
capitalist life. That is, to argue that we ought to take orthodox conceptions of money more seriously is to suggest not that we should celebrate
their descriptive credentials but rather that we should take them seriously as an expression of a particular imaginary that has certain effects.

In orthodox economic theory, no tension between fictitious and real
value is apparent. It is precisely because money is nothing but an accounting fiction, an arbitrary numerator to facilitate exchange, that it
can command respect as an objective, neutral measure and serve as a
source of unquestioned authority. In this way orthodox theory reproduces, in an uncritical and sanitized form, money's paradoxical character

as self-referential value. Contemporary money is a paradoxical combination of fiction and fact: we know it perfectly well to be a mere promise (if we knew the world would end tomorrow, money would be instantly worthless); and yet this in no way undermines its ability to function as entirely real value, as an objective standard for a wide range of human interactions. Every attempt to conceptually ground this certainty of practical economic reason in a value substance underlying the operations of money falters; we forever find ourselves being referred to further speculative, promissory operations. But in everyday life we do not experience any problems treating money as both a fiction and a fact (it is only when we need to give conceptual expression to our discontent with money that we begin to polarize these two aspects). Orthodox economic theory abstracts from the temporal dimension at play in this self-referential logic: it imagines that the problem of time can be reduced to the problem of coordination which arises in a barter economy and that it can be solved through a one-off designation of a common measure that essentially serves to detemporalize economic life. This allows orthodox economic theory to restate a paradoxical aspect of practical economic reason as a formal theoretical claim.

To explore money through the lens of its self-referentiality is to suggest that we might understand value as "plastic" rather than "elastic." Plasticity refers to the constitutive character of contingent associations, the way one connection inflects the generation and patterning of new connections and thus adjusts the course of history, allowing for the emergence of determinate entities in a world that has no external mover. Plasticity would be absent if identities were entirely impervious to outside influence, or if they were so fragile that even the slightest challenge led them to disintegrate altogether. A plastic identity (re)produces itself through continuous changes in relational form. At the limit, plasticity can mean an identity's overt lack of fixed, essential properties—implying a frontal challenge to a traditional, Aristotelian understanding of identity in terms of substance and accidental qualities or forms (Malabou 2000: 206). Contemporary money is highly plastic, lacking any essence and maintaining itself as an objective entity through the continuous transformation of the speculative connections that produce it. There is no discrete object that we can identify as the bearer of the dollar-identity, and in that sense money itself remains virtual, operating above all as an organizing force in a complex pattern of promissory relations. But even though this means that money has no essential core and is nothing but a configuration of symbolic forms, it also means that money operates with an undeniable nonrepresentational force: money is itself the thing that it represents. It refers beyond itself, back to itself, simply promising more of itself (cf. Rotman 1987: 5; Vogl 2015: 53–55).

These considerations echo tenets of Marxist value-form theory, which emerged from a recognition of the problems that plague the materialism of traditional Marxist value theory and its tendency to identify labor as the substance of value. Value-form theory has sought to go beyond such substantivism by emphasizing the constitutive role of the social and symbolic forms in which value appears (Rubin 1972; Elson 1979; Clarke 1982). Such approaches accommodate broader notions of labor that recognize its processual and mediated character, but they have had much difficulty articulating a qualitatively different perspective on the role of capitalism's value forms. That is, they have generally been unable to fully break with a conception of value as elastic (Knafo 2007). A persistent foundationalism tends to negate the critical purchase of the constructivist awareness that values are constituted through their symbolic forms. For instance, Clarke's (1988) work views neoliberal capitalism as driven by a speculative flight out of productive capital, and its portrayal of the dynamics of neoliberal finance resembles in important respects that of approaches it criticizes for their economic determinism and reliance on traditional base-superstructure metaphors.

Such persistent commitment to a substantivist theory of value is largely motivated by the conviction that to open the door fully to the constitutive role of value forms would be to invite relativism and subjectivism. That is to say, to conceive of the constitution of forms as *itself* the process whereby value is shaped and value measures are constituted—to view value as plastic rather than elastic—would seem to render value an arbitrary and tautological concept, providing no basis for distinguishing between fictions and facts, between irrationally speculative and sound significations of value. Such concerns reflect a continued tendency to understand form constitution as a process that is primarily epistemic, passively representational rather than performative and speculative. The role of representation is imagined in the way we tend to view the measurement of length: the meter is seen to constitute an independently determined unit of measure that simply registers the length value of an object external to it. It represents with a linearity and precision that can only obtain if a measure is independent from the object it measures. Value forms, however, work differently, as they are not defined in independence from the object being valued; they emerge from and constitute that object. The tendency in value-form theory to assess the salience of forms by their capacity for accurate representation suppresses the speculative moment and its ability to provoke the reality on whose dynamics it speculates. Form theory, in other words, has never proceeded to theorize fictitious forms in terms of their capacity to generate constitutive associations, affectively charged relations, and practical investments—that is, to induce the production of facticity (Negri 1999; Arvidsson 2009).

The inability of Marxist theory to disentangle itself from the essentializing legacy of substantivist understandings of value, money, and labor has always served as a source of legitimacy for idealist perspectives on economic life. Often framing their contributions as a critique of materialist determinism and looking instead to norms, discourse, and knowledge as alternative foundations, such perspectives place much greater emphasis on the idea that economic identities and structures are not materially pre-given but centrally dependent on the way people conceptually construct their world. In this way, the problematic of value has remained uncomfortably situated between materialism and idealism, between the poles of fetishized material labor and fetishized knowledge (Martin 2015).

This traditional division has been significantly rethought in autonomist approaches, which have sought to move beyond the opposition of
labor and knowledge to foreground the ways these dimensions are imbricated in contemporary capitalism. Of central importance here is the
emphasis on immanence, the impossibility of ontologically separating
the material and the ideal—a move that subverts a conception of social forms, norms, and standards as primarily representational and epistemic. In the era of immaterial labor, the assumption of an externality of
reality and its representation becomes less and less tenable; the measure
of value becomes more fully immanent. No longer simply a yardstick by
which something else is assessed, measure is produced in and through
the same process whereby the measured is constituted (Negri 1999).
But the implications of autonomist insights have remained somewhat
ambiguous. The immanence of knowledge and value is often portrayed
specifically as a characteristic of the post-Fordist era: it is the decline
of Fordism and its standardized methods of factory production that is
taken to have undermined abstract labor time as the organizing principle
of capitalist production by giving rise to immaterial forms of labor that
are increasingly difficult to represent or symbolize. In other words, the
immanence of value and measure is often understood by contrasting it
to an externality that supposedly prevailed under earlier periods of capitalist development, when the labor theory of value was still valid (e.g.,
Hardt and Negri 2001; Marazzi 2007). But to position the argument
in this way raises the question of what the novelty of Marx's critique
of political economy might have been in the first place. As Caffentzis
(2005) argues, Marx's critique of Ricardo's substantivist theory of labor
value rested precisely on the argument that capitalist valuation practices were not to be seen as external, timeless standards. His critique of
the utopian socialists was an insistence that there could be no objective
formal representation of a value substance, even in the capitalism of his
own time. Capital's measures and calculations are performative devices,
and Marx's *Capital* (1990 [1867]) can be read as an analysis of these calculative logics in a particular historical and geographical context (Bryan

and Rafferty 2013). Capital was not a passive appropriator of what had already been produced but played an active, constructive role in generating the very surplus value it was after.

My point here is neither to debate details of historical periodization nor to insist on a particular interpretation of Marx's *Capital*, but rather to draw attention to the fact that the interpretation of immanent measure as a decline or crisis of external measure inflects the autonomist theorization of the contemporary era in problematic ways. The most notable implication has been a certain postmodern valence that associates the shift from Fordism to post-Fordism with the impossibility of economic standardization and order and so downplays the ways the measurement and valuation of labor remain at the core of capitalist life (Adkins 2009). To assess the operation of contemporary value against the model of external measure and passive, linear registration is to pay insufficient attention to the distinctive dynamics and paradoxically generative character of an immanently generated standard (Clough et al. 2007; de Angelis and Harvie 2009; Böhm and Land 2009). The standard principally never prevents the emergence of new forms of speculative valuation—and in that sense the development of capitalism is an *ongoing* crisis of measure and representation (Bryan 2012). The lack of objective precision of endogenously generated standards means not that measuring and valuation become irrelevant but rather that the continuous valuation of speculative positions becomes all the more imperative. The permanent insufficiency of measure motivates relentless measuring; value's lack of ontological autonomy drives a dynamic of ongoing valuation (cf. Adkins and Lury 2011).

Value claims never transcend the speculative, promissory character of the interactions through which they emerged. They work not by creating an external standard but through "provoking" (Muniesa 2011: 32), through activating connections and prompting their reorganization around the validation of the speculative promise. Value is not given before it is signified: the signification of value is performative rather than passively representational, driven by the aim to elicit the generation of

the value that it claims to represent—it involves "prospecting for potential" (Adkins 2012: 625). Nor, crucially, does this process ever come
to a halt with the discovery of a "real economy" or fundamental values.
It forever works forward, by inflecting the ongoing generation of new
speculations and by inducing austerity, a subjective willingness to gear
the creation of new speculative positions and value forms to the validation of past investments. If the creation of fictitious forms instigates a
temporal dynamic that revolves around the prospect of actualizing the
virtual claim, the prospect of such bottom-line actuality always functions as an ever-receding horizon. The tension between speculation
and austerity can be seen as the affective structure of the plastic logic
of value, "the ghost in the financial machine" (Appadurai 2011), the
force field that holds together contingent assemblages of speculative
relations.

   If a kind of double movement is at work in capitalist life, this involves not a periodic oscillation between foundational values and speculative impulses but, instead, the constant need to respond productively
to speculative provocations, to reconstruct reality around a new connection that cannot be undone and has irrevocably altered how things
work (cf. Cooper and Konings 2015; Mitropoulos 2012). Along such
lines we can make sense of the post–financial crisis turn to austerity.
This turn occurred as commentators were still getting worked up about
the slowness with which regulators were following through on earlier
promises to implement more restrictive regulations, and it has been
widely interpreted in terms of the ability of financial elites to block the
Polanyian countermovement. Austerity policies are seen as producing
short-term benefits for "rentier interests" at the expense of the production of real value. Pursuing austerity instead of Keynesian demand stim-
ulation, financial and political elites are seen to deepen the recession and
to undermine the preconditions of economic growth and the foundations of profitability (Blyth 2013; Gamble 2014; Schui 2014). Although
it is certainly true that the austerity turn has promoted precarity and

accelerated the shift away from a world of consistent employment and steady paychecks, it is far from clear that this has undercut rather than promoted the valorization of capital. Insecurity, precarity, and instability have come to be characterized by their own internal logic as means of economic governance (Lorey 2015). From the view of the double movement suggested here, speculation and austerity should not be seen as part of the same disembedding movement: the austerity drive is the movement whereby capital secures its speculative investments and valorizes its fictions.

Speculation, Leverage, and Banking

Unless we develop our understanding of the constitution of value along such nonfoundational lines, we tend to end up in notoriously problematic debates about productive versus unproductive labor as a way to separate real from fictitious value—debates that only allow for moralistic and arbitrary solutions. Here it is worth returning to the key contribution of autonomist thought, namely the conceptual expansion of what counts as labor, often to the point where it is synonymous with practice, affect, or life, simply expressing the idea that no formal structure or symbolic order is ever sufficient unto itself and depends on the operation of a generative principle. The problem that is often seen to arise with that theoretical move is the difficulty of formulating a rigorous, nonarbitrary critique on such a vaporous basis. However, here I would like to suggest that we can follow the idea of form determination to its conclusion and critically conceptualize the active role of forms by examining their construction through mechanisms of leverage. Instead of being too concerned with ontological foundations and formulating critique in terms of the way our social forms and relations represent or deviate from those foundations, we may be better off simply asking how social forms work to give the practical activity of some so much more force and salience than that of others. Nobody's practices are inherently worth more than any other's, but some become positioned in social configurations such that their activity is greatly "leveraged" (Konings 2010). Actors try to format the patterns that connect them to others to get the greatest "bang for their buck," the greatest impact for a given amount of effort.

The concept of leverage is proposed here as a way to understand control and influence as operating immanently. Power never comes to rest in outside institutions or symbols but always works relationally and performatively, through the recursive activation of the operations and connections that compose it. Norms work not by governing actors from the outside but through the ways actors enlist others in operations that create a new system-level dynamic. In other words, the concept of leverage suggests a specific approach to the paradox that relational forms are immanent (produced by the field of interactions they operate in) yet constitutive (they change something in the field's structure). They do not simply increase the value of particular practices as assessed by a given external norm; rather, they shape the norm itself. Leverage, then, is the way we aim to give our fictitious projections a self-fulfilling, per-formative quality, how we seek to provoke the world into affirmatively responding to our speculative claims, to recruit the labor that will ensure their validation.

Leverage of course has an established meaning in economic theory, where it refers to the proportion of borrowed funds relative to one's own invested capital. A highly leveraged financial institution or system is one that operates on large amounts of debt. Orthodox finance theory thinks of leverage as more or less separate from the future-oriented judgment; actors choose what to invest in and then quantitatively amplify their exposure to the outcome by borrowing additional funds. Insofar as le-verage is understood as capable of affecting the nature of speculative activities itself, this is seen as occurring through price effects, the abil-ity to "move the market." Here I would like to suggest that we should not think of that possibility as an exceptional circumstance (as orthodox finance theory does) and to state the relevant principle more generally:

insofar as speculation is more than just gambling, it involves leveraging (cf. Allon 2015). After all, in a nonessentialist universe there is no capital, no fund of money that is originally owned and can be invested at will—we always already live on credit. There is no original speculation, only leveraging. Accordingly, leverage does not simply quantitatively amplify a speculative position but does something to shape the configuration of reality itself. If speculation is understood properly in its performative sense, leverage is an integral aspect of it.

To see this more clearly, we need to take a step back. Speculation itself is difficult to understand in the framework offered by mainstream economic and finance theory, as the latter works with a sanitized understanding of risk, one that purges it of uncertainty and assumes that the future is calculable provided we have the correct data and the right methods (Davidson 1991; Beckert 2016). This is an understanding of risk as nonperformative: actors are seen as facing a world that functions according to its own independent laws that can in principle be fully understood. If it is assumed, along such lines, that there are no inherent differences between the past and the future (that the present does not necessarily make a difference to the course of history, and that we can occupy a stationary moment that does not itself introduce new sources of change), we can hope to predict the future on the basis of the past—not of course in the sense that it is possible to correctly predict any specific future event, but in the sense that we can arrive at perfect probabilistic knowledge. The way we think about a lottery provides the relevant model here: precisely because randomness has been systematically produced and the influence of the subject has been systematically isolated, we can say that our knowledge is perfect.

But such redefinition of the lack of knowledge about the future as itself knowledge is hardly a convincing account of how we handle cognitive limitations in practice. Our aim is not simply to know a given normal distribution, but rather to shape norms as we make history. Crucially, this does not necessarily mean that we try to overcome the limits of our knowledge; it often simply means that we strategize around those

limits. This is where leveraging comes in as the organic complement
of speculation. It is a response to the practical problem of "how to use
the uncertainty of the future, to exploit it without being paralysed by
it" (Esposito 2011: 20). Leverage has a preemptive quality: it responds
to the fact that we can never fully know the future and need to rely on
strategies that can feed off that permanent element of uncertainty. It
effects a shift in perspective, from one that would predict the future to
one that aims to make investments that will bend the production of the
future around one's own position. Leverage involves the effort to position oneself as the focal point of the interactive logic of speculation, as
an attractor in the social field. It is a way to inflect the production of
norms and so to become a factor in or precondition for other actors'
decision-making capacities.

The way I leverage off others' uncertainty is by inducing them to invest in my promises as a way to hedge against the uncertainty they face.
Through a leveraging operation, I seek to insinuate myself into the way
others comprehend their own conditions of reproduction. That way,
when others respond to unanticipated circumstances and unimagined
problems, they are likely to draw on the resources that my normative
position makes available, thereby fortifying my centrality in the social
fabric. To highlight the leveraging logic of specularity thus shifts the
emphasis away from the ability to accurately calculate risk toward how
actors seek to institute their own promises as the relevant unit of calculation. Economic power depends not just on knowing but equally on
being known in a context of pervasive uncertainty; it derives from the
ability to serve as a central point of reference in the specular logic of
contingent claims. In other words, leverage is not just about increasing
my exposure to the world, but about increasing the world's exposure to
and investment in the risk that I am taking. It is a distinctly secular form
of sovereignty, bound up not with the possibility of transcending the
ordinary field of risk but with the possibility of "transforming [one's]
own risks into the dangers of all others" (Vogl 2014: 153).

A pure form of leverage is approximated in the practice of banking (Sgambati 2015). Its primary aim is to continuously borrow and lend and to confer currency on the obligations it issues in doing so. The question of exactly how to invest is often secondary—and as we saw in the run-up to the financial crisis of 2007–8, it is perfectly possible for banks to have incentives to invest in obligations they realize are unlikely to ever be repaid. In other words, a bank has overtly no substantive goal, no purpose other than to effect a hierarchizing movement whereby its commitments come to occupy a special position in the overall configuration of social promises. A bank's promises function as a standard against which the value of other promises is measured—that is, as money.

The viability of modern banking is premised on the element of ineradicable uncertainty in the dynamics of economic interaction. Without uncertainty, we would have no need for either banks or the promises they issue. Banking operations make the unknowability of the future manageable: they transform a situation where we lack sufficient knowledge to make decisions into a situation where we can think probabilistically. The promises that a bank generates institute an economic norm, a standard of value. Bank money functions as something like a time-storage device, a means to keep options and possibilities open (Opitz and Tellmann 2015: 113). Money is the most speculative object we deal with in life (fully promissory, indisputably useless except for the promise it holds), but also the most objective and reliable form of risk navigation that we have. Holding money is our least uncertain bet. Of course, modern citizens no longer think of their money as bank obligations; they think of it as legal tender, guaranteed by the state. But money has always remained bank money in a crucial sense: insofar as the state has a "money printing press," this is fully bound up with the internalization of banking functions into the machinery of government. The creation of a national currency can only happen through the unification of a banking system through a central bank.

Banking never escapes the logic of risk, and money never functions
as an absolute standard of value that prevents the emergence of alternative or competing processes of valuation. The contingent character of
a bank's operations becomes apparent when people lose trust in bank
promises and withdraw their funds—what is known as a "run on the
bank." But we should be alert to the fact that these recurrent dynamics
of leveraging and deleveraging have often played a productive role and
have been the motor behind further financial organization. Of course,
failure can just mean failure pure and simple, sheer disintegration. But
in modern capitalism it often enough doesn't: once a bank has positioned itself as a key part of the infrastructure of social life at large, its
failure or merely the threat of it will activate forces that seek to secure it.
At work here is essentially a too-big-to-fail dynamic: when large, highly
leveraged financial institutions come under pressure, valuation comes
to be governed by the logic of bailout and austerity. In a great deal of
political economy scholarship, neither of these latter phenomena are
properly conceptualized. They are typically depicted as exceptional features of financial governance or as irrational policies, rarely as system-
atic features of a financial regime that has evolved historically. Yet the
rearrangement of debt and the redistribution of payment pressures have
always been at the heart of both the business and the governance of
banking (Baecker 1991: 55). To say that leverage allows financial institutions to expose society to the risk they take on means that they are in a
position to shift risk away from themselves and onto others. As modern
subjects we are all too familiar with the dynamic of a system-level crisis
that requires us to respond productively to events we feel we had no
role in producing.

The way capitalist development is affected by the dynamics of leveraging and deleveraging, the expansion and contraction of credit, has
always been a principal point of reference for the critique of orthodox
economics. Post-Keynesian theory, the most prominent contemporary
representative of this focus, conceptualizes that logic in terms of the periodic expansion of speculative credit and fictitious capital and how that

distorts capitalism's underlying production structures (Keen 2011; Palley 2013; Tymoigne and Wray 2014). An unfortunate conceptual slide is at work here: from the acknowledgement of the ineradicability of risk, fluctuation, and volatility to a cyclical theory of history that precisely negates the productive role of contingency and is only able to view the speculative engagement of risk as a divergence from foundations. Whereas the former suggests a notion of the "eternal return" of contingency in a Nietzschean sense—that is, there is no external instance to confer absolute value or eternal life on our constructions, or as Deleuze puts it, "It is not being that returns but rather the returning itself that constitutes being" (1986: 48)—the latter negates that critical insight by positing a model of largely predictable periodicity.

If post-Keynesian theory positions itself as an alternative economic theory, the cyclical model receives a more general and politicized expression in interdisciplinary fields such as economic sociology and political economy, where the idea of cyclical temporality is often put forward as an alternative to structuralist or teleological approaches. It is epitomized by the Polanyian perspective, which views history as governed by the alternation of phases governed by foundational value with phases that give free rein to speculation. According to this model, the unshackling of markets and rampant speculation during the early twentieth century were responsible for the interwar breakdown of capitalism; the post–New Deal and postwar state responded to this by expanding protections and limiting the reach of speculative markets and restoring the rule of fundamental value; neoliberalism has sought to reverse this trend and to disembed markets from their institutional constraints; and the inevitable crisis that this unbalanced expansion of finance will produce will once again force a return to foundations. Polanyian perspectives interpret the expansion of finance under neoliberalism as reflecting the inability or reluctance of capital to profitably ground itself in the world of real value, work, and production, exploring instead the world of fictitious profits. Not only do such perspectives miss the fact that financial expansion is deeply imbricated with the restructuring of

work and subjectivity; they are also formulated against the background
of a highly nostalgic (and in many respects misleading) image of the
early postwar era as an order that served to suppress the role of speculation and finance.

Particularly problematic here is the tendency to see the welfare state
as external to the risk dynamics of capitalism and to view its effects in
terms of the decommodification of labor. Conceptually inclined histo-
rians such as Ewald (1986) and Castel (2003) have insisted, by contrast,
that the midtwentieth-century welfare state was never external to the
market but rather central in organizing its risk logic. The welfare state
represented less a "balance" between a capitalist economy and a social-
democratic polity than an integration of the population into the mechanisms of capitalism in ways that transformed those mechanisms at their
core. If the work of these authors has focused mostly on Europe, such
insights hold a fortiori for the United States, whose welfare state was
always a capitalist institution in more overt ways. Class compromise was
brokered not through the suppression of finance but precisely through
its state-sponsored expansion. The most significant aspects of this
were the creation of the so-called government-sponsored enterprises,
which supported the ability of the financial system to flexibly extend
various forms of household credit; and the institution of deposit insurance, which undercut the phenomenon of bank runs and so permitted
a normalization of the role of commercial banks in everyday life. The
post–New Deal era saw the progressive socialization of American workers into the mechanisms of credit and debt. The emergence of a Fordist
regime of full employment and a living wage was never the foundation
of an unindebted life or the suppression of finance, as many now imagine, but was precisely the basis on which households entered into contracts of consumer and mortgage credit. In an important sense, the New
Deal was a key step in the direction of what under neoliberalism has
become more recognizable as "the capitalization of almost everything"
(Leyshon and Thrift 2007), the measurement of human capacities in

terms of their ability to provide a flow of revenues (cf. Nitzan and Bichler 2009: 158).

Of course, access to credit was far from universal, the principal exclusionaries being women and ethnic minorities, especially African Americans. As these and other groups began to challenge institutionalized exclusions, this put considerable pressure on the mechanisms of American finance. The growing demand for credit could not be met within the institutional parameters of the New Deal system, and gave rise to the development of what since the financial crisis of 2007–8 has come to be known as a "shadow banking system"—composed of financial institutions that function on the principle of banking leverage even if the liquid promises they issue do not qualify as legal tender and are not insured (Gorton 2012; Ricks 2016). This placed the American state in an increasingly contradictory relation to the financial system. On the one hand, social and political order was deeply bound up with the ability of the financial system to expand the provision of credit to both existing and new constituencies. Indeed, even as the shadow banking system made ample use of the securitization facilities offered by the government-sponsored enterprises, the American state always found itself forced to support their ongoing expansion. On the other hand, these developments entailed a return to dynamics of leveraging and deleveraging that placed the Fed in a difficult position: policies that could contain the most serious effects of instability fed accelerating inflation, whereas attempts to tighten credit would quickly lead to a new expansion of shadow banking activity and renewed instability. The American state was trying to control with one hand a dynamic that it found itself forced to continue feeding with the other hand. Its policies were entangled in the workings of the American banking system in a way that it was able to recognize as problematic, but this recognition did not automatically translate into an ability to do something about the problem. The turn to neoliberalism should be situated in this context.

Financial Governance and Neoliberal Reason

Critiques of neoliberalism have revolved around the argument that the unshackling of markets has brought not a world of neutrality and efficiency but a dramatic expansion of financial speculation out of all proportion to economic fundamentals, resulting in instability and crisis. On such a reading, neoliberalism is an attempt to return to classic free-market liberalism, which has forgotten the lessons of the interwar period when the project of laissez-faire liberalism revealed itself to be irrational, unsustainable, and destructive. In this way, critics of neoliberalism have too often focused on rejecting its most literal, surface-level claims about neutrality and efficiency. They have spent relatively little time trying to decipher the imaginary that such notions express, and as a consequence they have had great difficulty taking neoliberalism seriously as—what Foucault calls—a "rationality of governmental practice" (2008 [1979]: 13).

Recent years have seen a reinvigoration of debates about the nature of neoliberalism. An important factor here has been the translation and publication of Foucault's late lectures at the Collège de France (especially 2008 [1979] but also 2007 [1978] and 2003 [1976]), where he argues that neoliberalism should not be seen as a simple revival of classic liberalism, and that the critical analysis of neoliberalism should not set too much store by the orthodox image of the market as a Smithian transactional structure. Whereas classic liberalism merely sought to remove the institutional barriers impeding the natural unfolding of the utilitarian logic of market exchange, neoliberalism embraces a speculative orientation toward the future as an organizing principle. Far from naturalizing the market, it is fully aware of the need to actively construct the institutions of capitalist order (Dardot and Laval 2014). It intuits speculation as a productive, ordering impulse and brings the engagement of uncertainty into the logic of governance. Whereas classic liberalism was primarily interested in discounting the uncertainty of the future, neoliberalism valorizes the outer edges of calculability, the incalculable and unpredictable (Cooper 2011). This means that neoliberal reason is characterized by a concern with temporality that remains absent or suppressed in classic economic liberalism and in neoclassical economics. It does not imagine money as a simple one-off solution to the barter problem, but views finance as a way to construct an unknown future. It is more interested in financialization than commodification (Cooper 2008: 10), more taken with the promises and prospects of investment than the immediate utility of consumption, more engaged with the generative role of speculation than the stasis of general equilibrium (cf. Vogl 2015: 57).

This is certainly not to deny that orthodox images of the market as an innocuous mediator and of money as a neutral transactional device have been central to neoliberalism. Rather, I am arguing that it has a more reflexive relation to those images than its progressive critics tend to realize. Neoliberal reason is not constrained by a literal reading of the way neoclassical theory has formalized the orthodox economic imaginary—that is, it is more engaged with the spirit than the letter of that imaginary. The relevant difference can be brought out with reference to Hayek's work, which Foucault considered to hold important clues to the nature of neoliberalism, even though he was not able to examine that Hayekian angle in much detail (Gane 2014). Whereas neoclassical theory suppresses the ongoing role of speculation in economic life, Hayek's work thematizes it. Rejecting epistemological positivism, it insists that any hope for complete and certain knowledge is illusory, that ordering through centralized knowledge is principally impossible, and that uncertainty and not-knowing are constitutive and ineradicable aspects of the problem of economic value and coordination. But those insights never led him to abandon the orthodox tenet of market neutrality. In Hayek's work the image of neutrality comes to serve as a regulatory horizon, always receding and forever demanding an intensified commitment to the uncertainties and imperatives of the economy. Neoliberalism's rationality of risk is, to borrow Critchley's (2007) phrase, "infinitely demanding."

The idea of neutrality may at first sight not seem like a particularly promising candidate for the organizing element of an imaginary—it would seem too bland to inspire the mind or fire up our senses, at least compared with more explicitly political narratives or religious imagery. But here it is crucial to appreciate the affective and ethical force that this distinctly modern notion commands, and the powerful ways it exerts organizing effects on our psychological economy. To say that the modern economic imaginary pivots on the idea of neutrality is to underscore that even as the subject readily intuits the inevitability of risk, she remains deeply invested in the fantasy that she may one day be able to observe that logic from an external perspective, enabling her to stage clean, surgical interventions and so to confer on her own life an uncontentious, unchallenged security. The fantasy here is one of immunity—that one day we may be able to enjoy the benefits and freedom offered by contingency without experiencing its downside. The image of neutrality thus plays on the distinctly secular promise that we can move through risk beyond risk, that if we play our cards right and make the correct investments we may provide our lives with nonspeculative foundations. Modernity destroys a particular ("transcendent") kind of idealism, but it fosters another ("transcendental") variety. If much of what we do is motivated precisely by the awareness that we cannot count on outside forces or guarantees, the idea of neutrality relates to the fantasy that we can provide those guarantees ourselves—that we can diagnose and remove our blind spots and that the logic of specularity will overcome its need to play itself out in real time, resulting in the self-transparency of the here and now.

This imaginary works on what we might think of as a Kantian leap from the awareness of contingency to the regulative fantasy that we may end up occupying a neutral view from nowhere in this life. The orthodox conception of money expresses this fantasy as a formal proposition about the nature of money; it reduces the problem of time and uncertainty to a technical problem of coordination and views money as a simple, transparent solution to the latter, as a mere "expediter of transactions" (Minsky 1982: 61). The monetary standard is seen as fully arbitrary, generated through a speculative act that institutes a linear, objective measure and so moves us beyond speculation. Money is imagined as akin to an ideal language: a perfect vehicle for expressing ourselves without ever distorting or changing our meaning, establishing a perfect correspondence between essence and appearance, substance and form, value and price. To simply dismiss this as an irrational idea would be a somewhat moralistic response that ignores the constitutive effects of this fantasy, its ability to generate an affective charge and serve as a binding force, as an unimagined version of the functional cohesion that it imagines. Neoliberalism recognizes and deploys this affective logic, invoking the prospect of secure life to motivate the intensified engagement of risk. The conception of money as a neutral technology is accordingly by no means confined to professional economists and central bankers, but enjoys considerable popular traction and a great deal of commonsensical appeal. Especially in the American context, this is borne out by a long history of popular republican sentiments and movements that have had the achievement of market neutrality as one of their core objectives (Goebel 1997; Ritter 1999; Postel 2009). Republicanism imagines an economic order based on decentralized markets that offer a bulwark against accumulations of power and arbitrary, unjustified authority. The large banks and corporations that do not fit this picture of the market are always viewed as external sources of corruption, and the task is to purify the market and restore its neutrality. This often gives the populist politics of republicanism a highly utopian or counterfactual flavor; the very fact that capitalist life is so patently at odds with the republican image of the market becomes the reason for a reinforcement of attachment to the fantasy. Neoliberalism's ability to align itself with such discourses has been central to its success (Kazin 1998).

The reason much critical thinking about economic life has been unable to recognize and critically penetrate this imaginary is that it has often itself remained hostage to the conceptual logic of the Kantian leap, forever ready to seize on the observation of contingency to espouse a rationalist constructivism. Kantian idealism can be seen as the specter that haunts modern thinking about economic life: widely disavowed but forever rearing its head in the most surprising places. It never tires of rediscovering contingency and complexity, and takes such findings as occasions for a return to an idealist essentialism and a revalorization of a politics of discursive consensus and communal values. This is evident almost everywhere in critical work on political economy and economic sociology, in the guise of an all-too-familiar mode of argument that takes the emphasis on contingency as the occasion for a reaffirmation of an intentionalist constructivism.

What the cyclical model of capitalist history has difficulty acknowledging is that neoliberalism is a reflexive response to the genetic modifications that capitalism underwent over the course of the twentieth century as large segments of the population were integrated into its financial logic and as the state became fully implicated in that dynamic. Even as neoliberalism was very much a response to the state's perceived ambitions for social engineering and caretaking, its practical concerns were always driven by a sense that the state could *not* simply be shrunk or rolled back; further, the practical commitments of neoliberal politics were never premised on the possibility of a clean break with the past. Of course, the notion that neoliberalism is simply about expanding the market at the expense of the state has by now been criticized widely. But such arguments are often pulled in either of two problematic directions: one is the idea that the impact of neoliberalism on the operation of the state has been highly limited, and the other involves an emphasis on the state's authoritarian role in enforcing neoliberalism in the vein of a Schmittian exceptionalism. Both of these miss the reflexive element in neoliberalism, its ability to position itself as a philosophy of governance that precisely recognizes the state's inability to separate itself from the economic and social processes it needs to govern. In that sense, neoliberalism is a mode of thinking that has at least an intuitive appreciation—and often an explicit awareness—of the limits of rational constructivism, a theme that is at the heart of Hayek's work.

The problem the American state was facing at the end of the 1970s was that it needed to make adjustments in the dynamics of a banking system with whose operation it had become deeply entangled, and that it lacked the instruments to extricate itself. Read along such lines, neoliberalism is an intervention in the logic of contingency and speculation that precisely does *not* take itself to be outside of that logic. This Foucauldian insight has been made more specific by Ewald, who suggests that the development of risk governance can be understood as a transition from defensive orientations that are primarily concerned with organizing insurance for the impact of future events, to more purposely proactive orientations that work on "an ethic of the necessary decision in a context of uncertainty" (2002: 294). Whereas the former remain within the logic of the normal distribution, the latter push into areas of risk that challenge meaningful actuarial calculation. With respect to modern financial governance, we can note that even though it has always aligned governmental operations with the logic of risk, until well into the twentieth century this had a rather passive and reactive orientation, accommodating rather than using the dynamics of speculation. It is here that neoliberalism intervenes, insisting that government proactively engage the speculative dimension of financial life.[1]

As Ewald (2002: 285) emphasizes, this shift should be understood not as a clean replacement of one principle of government with another but precisely as a repositioning within a historically grown logic of financial risk. Neoliberalism does not imagine itself capable of conjuring a future from mere fictions, but proposes a way to handle historically grown commitments and expectations. The speculative orientation of neoliberal governance always articulates with the continued operation of normalizing forces and principles of insurance. In other words, neoliberalism intuits the potential ordering effects of the engagement of the outer reaches of risk, the self-organizing mechanisms that can be set in motion through the active engagement of uncertainty. Neoliberal discourses during the 1960s and 1970s were marked by a sense that the secular decline of capitalist order was in many ways a more

serious danger than its cataclysmic collapse. Accordingly, a key aspect
of neoliberal politics is to preemptively engage potential threats before
they undermine the system in a more pernicious way (Massumi 2014).
Marked by a keen awareness of the role of failure in the construction of
operational norms, it seeks to proactively enforce adjustment, allowing
crises and instability to play a productive role. Neoliberal policies are
oriented not to the prevention of failure but rather to its preemption—
in the dual sense of the word, both activating it and forestalling its most
serious consequences. The (in)famous Volcker shock of 1979, a decisive
moment in the making of neoliberal capitalism in which the newly ap-
pointed Federal Reserve chairman Paul Volcker shifted to a new set of
policy targets and operating procedures, was not motivated by a precise
understanding of its consequences; his policy turn was fully speculative,
provoking failure in the anticipation that this would activate some of
the system's ordering, self-organizing mechanisms.

The turn to neoliberalism reconfigured the American state's relation
to and role in the operation of the banking system in a way that made
some major governance problems more manageable. If this found its
most visible expression in the conquest of inflation, it never involved a
suppression of financial dynamism—indeed, the neoliberal system after
the Volcker shock was characterized by a far higher degree of financial instability than before. By abruptly refusing to accommodate the
expansion of credit any longer, the Volcker shock essentially invited
a dramatic expansion of the shadow banking system, which meant a
full-fledged return to the dynamics of leveraging and deleveraging. It
was always clear that the American state would have to play a role in
containing the fallout of these dynamics. But the informal institutionalization of a regime of too-big-to-fail policies essentially replaced an
inflationary form of across-the-board support with a much more selective application of government guarantees and insurance facilities.
The growth of the neoliberal shadow banking system has been fed by
the rapid growth of personal and household debt amid stagnant wage
growth, the erosion of job security, and repeated cuts in public income

protection. Neoliberal financial governance practices have been bound up not with a naïve belief in market efficiency but rather with a logic of speculation, bailout, and austerity.

Critical scholarship has had considerable difficulty recognizing this rationality of financial governance. Viewing neoliberalism as a naïve belief in the self-regulating properties of markets, it has failed to engage the ways neoliberal policies have in fact been able to mobilize their own specific sources of cohesion and resilience. It has been prone to prematurely announcing the demise of neoliberalism, and it has tended to view the persistence of neoliberalism as an exceptional phenomenon, a deviation from a normative model of mixed governance. Although the failure of a progressive re-embedding movement to materialize in the wake of the financial crisis has led many scholars to devote greater attention to the question of neoliberalism, this wave of scholarship has so far relied heavily on instrumentalist accounts of the role of ideas and elite interests in politics (Crouch 2011; Mirowski 2013; Streeck 2014). On such a reading, neoliberalism's date of expiry has long passed and it is only held together by political tricks and schemes. It is therefore important to consider how we might understand neoliberalism even if we assume little about the ability of capitalist elites to capture state institutions or the minds of policymakers—that is, even if we assume that state personnel is not necessarily corrupted by private interests but primarily disposed to stabilize the economic system, relying on an imaginary that is not readily reducible to a specific set of interests or ideas. In other words, we need to conceptualize a distinctive neoliberal political rationality, something that deserves to be termed "neoliberal reason" (Peck 2010)—understood not as formal ideational consistency but as a degree of cohesion at the level of practice and the imaginaries that orient it (Brown 2015).[2]

This book develops an understanding of neoliberalism's rationality in terms of the paradoxical temporality that is engendered by the affectively charged tension between the necessity of speculation and the anticipation of certainty. The preemptive orientation of neoliberal subjectivity and governance is motivated by a concern to secure the future, while the recurrent failure to achieve such nonspeculative security only serves to intensify the commitment to the engagement of risk—resulting in a Hayekian imperative of ceaseless speculation in the name of economic neutrality. But although this book aligns itself with work in both social theory and political economy that foregrounds questions of futurity, it places a great deal of emphasis on the fact that this logic centrally involves a reactionary moment—also present in Hayek's work, which frequently reminds the modern subject of the importance of tradition and custom in navigating the uncertain future. The element of reaction becomes apparent at moments of crisis. At such times, society has no option but to reinforce the nodal points of financial interconnectedness, historically generated patterns of leverage and power. The moment of bailout is characterized by an absence of meaningful choice: intense un-certainty about what the future has in store comes to coincide with a compelling certainty as to what needs to be done. The future simply im-poses itself, albeit in the shape of the past. The logic of preemption now manifests itself in yet a third sense, as a foreclosure on the future. And yet bailouts do not simply stabilize the system in a straightforward way or effect a return to foundations. The state can only give the banks time, not ironclad guarantees of value; bailouts are themselves highly specula-tive interventions that involve a great deal of dislocation and demand a response, rekindling the preemptive rationality even as they make appar-ent its contradictions.

CHAPTER 1

Foundationalism and Self-Referentiality

Money is nothing but a symbol, a fictitious stand-in for something else that is yet to arrive. After all, taken by itself, money is useless; people would have no reason to hold pieces of paper or even purely notional electronic accounting entries unless they felt that those signs referred beyond themselves and stood for something else. But it turns out to be extremely difficult to specify the objective ground of money: every attempt to indicate the foundational value of which money is imagined to be the symbolic expression refers us to other symbolic operations. And yet this inability to arrive at a substance underlying the value of money does not in any way undermine our sense that it is fully real. Even though we cannot define money beyond its fictitious and promissory character, this does not erode our sense that it represents entirely real value—indeed, *is* value. Money certainly can and does refer beyond its current self but always relates to its environment in terms of the potential for monetization that the environment holds. Monetary signs, then, are self-referential, capable of becoming the facts they symbolize (Deutschmann 2015: 382). We can and should study how this works, but any attempt to define value *outside* this paradoxical self-referential loop is bound to entail a moment of arbitrariness, a decision that reflects primarily our own reluctance to follow the self-referential movement of financial value.

Whereas orthodox economic theory unreflexively reproduces the paradoxical self-referentiality of monetary value, heterodox and critical theories insist on a clear distinction between real and fictitious money and so turn a blind eye to our intuitive certainty that money works as self-referential value. Seen from a heterodox angle, to emphasize the self-referentiality of monetary value would be to commit the fallacy of economism—that is, to assume that the economy is a self-sufficient entity, an autonomous, self-expanding system that requires no external supports or inputs. What makes an analysis economistic, in this perspective, is the inability to recognize that financial structures are not self-founding or self-regulating but require external foundations. Although there are many differences among the interdisciplinary social science fields studying economic life, the critique of economic determinism is central to how they have come to understand themselves. The critique of economism has been closely allied with the critique of speculation, which is understood as driven by an irrational belief in self-referentiality. Speculative practices, it is argued, are problematic because they fail to observe the importance of foundational values and do not properly distinguish between irrational and sound forms of value, between fiction and fact.

It is important to get a clear perspective on the reasoning here: the critique of self-referentiality is premised on an ontological foundationalism. Of course, it is widely and casually assumed that the critique of self-referentiality is concomitant precisely with a *rejection* of foundationalism—the one is imagined to imply the other, and both arguments tend be rolled into a critique of economism. But there is considerable conceptual sloppiness at work here, which serves to obscure the fact that the critique of speculation is in fact premised on a notion of real value. What is so remarkable about the present state of heterodox thinking about economic life is that the critique of speculation as a divergence from foundations has become closely allied with the critique of economic essentialism, with little registration of the deep tension between the two.

This book argues that it is precisely the inability to think self-referentiality properly that binds the heterodox critique to foundationalism; viewing self-referentiality through a non-essentialist lens obviates the need to locate phenomena in external grounds or substances. To this end, the book pursues the lead of Luhmann's understanding of self-reference. For Luhmann, it makes little sense to doubt that there exist self-referential, self-regulating systems, entities oriented to reproducing themselves into the future. To talk meaningfully about biological, human, or social life is to assume that such systems exist. Luhmann does not take self-referentiality as a positive property of systems or as an inherent power (the kind of essentializing conception that is the target of the critique of economism); it does not entail the literal closure of a system (whether a fully effective cognitive framing or a system's material ability to dispense with its environment) but only and ever an operational closure (Borch 2011: 23–24), which occurs when an assemblage of elements becomes organically oriented to reproducing itself (or in the language of Foucault [2007 (1978)], when it comes to be characterized by a "security dispositif" [cf. Luhmann 1995: 312]). For Luhmann, an emphasis on self-referentiality is the only way to do something useful with the idea of postfoundational theory, a theory appropriate to a society that is able to understand itself in terms of risk, and its institutions as contingent constructions. Whereas a Kantian problematic forever revolves around the external conditions that make particular phenomena and our knowledge of them possible, Luhmann's work is concerned precisely with obviating such modernized metaphysics and instead seeks to understand how systems endogenously generate their conditions of possibility. To view life through the lens of self-referentiality, then, is a way of framing the paradoxical phenomenon of determinate things coming into being in a world that has no external mover.

To draw on Luhmann to formulate a critical perspective is hardly an obvious move. In the English-speaking academic world, Luhmann was for a long time known primarily through his debate with Habermas (Habermas and Luhmann 1971), leaving the impression of being a conservative defender of system integration and having little interest in the quest of Frankfurt School critical theory to spot openings for political reform and change. The considerations offered here follow Moeller's (2012) suggestion that it is worth uncovering a "radical Luhmann," who does not so much retreat from critique but rather provides us with new critical resources. For Frankfurt School critical theory since its reconstruction by Habermas (1981), critique has had a strongly external character; normative judgments and moral commitments are seen as rooted in discursive practices that enjoy a degree of separation from the material pressures imposed and instrumental reason fostered by the economic sphere. For Luhmann, normativity never has such independence; it is only meaningfully thought about with reference to the functional requirements of system reproduction. From a Luhmannian perspective, Habermasian discourse ethics is little more than dressing up moralistic idealism as critical insight (Rasch 2002: 10). Especially when it comes to the subject of this book, this is hardly an unfair assessment. In the work of contemporary Frankfurt School representatives, a growing emphasis on communitarian or civic-liberal principles of interaction is accompanied by a steadily declining ability to offer penetrating readings of the capitalist economic structures whose oppressive operation and colonizing dynamics are taken to require the need for critical interventions in the first place. The tendency of key figures in the recent generation of Frankfurt School critical theory to align themselves with Polanyi's work and embrace the notion of the double movement (or some variation thereof) is therefore hardly coincidental but rather represents the logical endpoint of a particular way of thinking (e.g., Fraser 2013; Honneth 2014).[1]

Before exploring Luhmann's contribution in more detail, we need to appreciate the theoretical context in which his work should be seen as intervening. Systems thinking in the social sciences has always been much more prominently represented through Parsons's (1951) structural functionalism. The latter provided the methodological framework for the postwar social sciences and rationalized the specific division of labor among them. It viewed society as composed of a number of (sub) systems, each characterized by its own action orientation that could be studied through a specific kind of disciplinary knowledge—"Parsons' Pact." To a high degree this framework was organized around the growing importance of the economy in modern society, which had created a particular problem of order. The instrumentally rational, individualized actor was viewed as not organically disposed to the production of social and political order, and was therefore seen to require embedding in cultural and political frameworks of shared norms and values. In the post–World War Two context, the concern with social integration went hand in hand with the idea that any deviations from the values of liberal democracy could be treated as "social problems," reflecting not deepseated social tensions but accidental failures of integration.

The transformation of the social sciences over the past decades is of course far more complex than could be accurately described here. Yet for the specific focus of this book, we can characterize the shift fairly precisely as a rejection of totalizing explanations—and in particular any version of economic determinism—and the commitment to a more pluralist perspective that emphasizes the complex and contingent effects of specific institutional, political, and cultural factors.[2] This "new pluralism"—which we might call it to distinguish it from earlier forms of pluralism—places great emphasis on the provisional and contingent nature of any overarching order. Although the Parsonian paradigm had always been intensely concerned with the idea that economic action could not in and of itself serve as the basis of a coherent political order, the image of modernization it relied on was nonetheless a highly benevolent one, featuring productive forces of functional specialization that simply needed stabilizing. Whereas Parsonian modernization theory had given Weber an optimistic twist, the new pluralism returned to the tragic Weber, who was preoccupied with the irrationality of economic reason and who saw secular progress and moral decline as going hand in hand. In the new pluralism, the problem isn't just that external inputs are needed to stabilize economic rationality, but rather that the

irrational and expansionary aspects of (in particular financial) markets
pose a consistent threat to the possibility of order.

The new pluralism thus positions the logic of the social more
squarely in opposition to the logic of the economic, and in this way
it has remained caught in the very terms of Parsons' Pact. As a result,
entirely contrary to its stated intentions, its conceptual thrust has always been a rather essentializing one. On the one hand, money and
finance come to figure as external forces, driven not by substantive
ends and values but by a systemic, self-expansionary logic that is not
itself explained except negatively (that is, in terms of the irrationality of
financial capital's speculative impulses). On the other hand, the problematic of ordering becomes centrally organized around the possibility
of protecting against such external forces of fragmentation, and we find
a much stronger emphasis on the autonomy of institutions, that is, the
idea that order is an intentional construction fabricated by distinct actors, ideas, and strategies.

Such tendencies are particularly evident in the growing prominence
of Polanyi's work. At its heart is a critique of the notion that markets
can be self-regulating; it is centrally concerned with the tendency of
markets to become disembedded from their environment, the unsustainable nature of such trends, and the need to re-embed markets by
restoring limits and foundations. This reasoning reflects an elastic
model of value, which distinguishes between real and fictitious forms
of value and sees the tendency of finance to exceed its natural limits
as creating a quantitative imbalance that must sooner or later lead to
financial collapse. Polanyian scholars would of course readily reject the
suggestion that they rely on a foundationalist understanding of value.
But it is crucial to appreciate that this defense is typically premised on
a reduction of the problem of foundationalism to the problems with
Marxist materialism (in particular the labor theory of value)—and it is
telling that much Polanyian scholarship begins by outlining its differences from Marxist materialism, as if that were the only form of essentialism to guard against. For all practical intents and purposes, the

Polanyian framework is fully organized around the idea that economic life can work only on the basis of external conditions of possibility. At work here is a Kantian leap, which takes the critique of materialist foundationalism and the rediscovery of contingency as the occasion for a leap into an idealist foundationalism (Cooper and Konings 2015). Furthermore, this idealist foundationalism all too readily relapses into a materialist foundationalism of its own; as much as Polanyian thought is predicated on the rejection of Marxist materialism, its assessments of the stability of social life are profoundly shaped by the contrast between speculative finance and the "real economy," and by an infatuation with the manufacturing economy of the Fordist era. In the meantime, the expansionary tendencies and systemic properties of the financial system are explained entirely in negative terms, as investors' inability to recognize foundations and limits and to attribute reality to fictions. While market disembedding is said to be unsustainable in the long run, we find no plausible explanation for why it occurs in the first place. Polanyian thought revolves around a systemic, self-referential moment that it is unable to theorize.

CHAPTER 2

Constructions and Performances

One way of capturing these problems is to say that the constructivist strain of thinking that runs so prominently through the new pluralism (e.g., Blyth 2003; Seabrooke 2007; Hay 2016) has often been somewhat abortive. It relies heavily on what Knodt, in her introduction to Luhmann's *Social Systems*, refers to as "popularized versions of constructivism that attempt to sell, under a new name, old forms of epistemological idealism" (1995: xv). It has taken the form of an intentionalist constructivism, which assumes acts of construction to be self-transparent and views ideas and norms as working in linear and predictable ways (cf. Palan 2000; Bucher 2014). Complexity and contingency are introduced via an ontological pluralism, an insistence on the operation of a multiplicity of norms and ideas—rather than as conditions at the heart of the operation of norms. At work here is the unjustified (and, as I will argue, unjustifiable) assumption that constructivism and pluralism go hand in hand or even should be seen as interchangeable theoretical commitments.

Much of human life, assessed by such an idealist conception of normativity, is obviously not constructed. Consequently, even as social scientists have conceded that social life is constructed, made by the interaction of ideas and subjects, many of them have remained deeply resistant to the idea that social life is constructed "all the way down." The literature has revolved around the need to "balance" ideal and material factors, the emphasis on constructedness with an acknowledgment of hard facts that simply exist (e.g., Abdelal et al. 2010). What constructivism in political economy and economic sociology often boils down to is a certain sensitivity to nonmaterial factors such as ideas and identities, which are investigated through an empiricism that treats as positive facts the very phenomena that it claims are discursively and socially constructed, performative and observer-dependent. The result has been a definite defanging of the idea of construction: it has morphed from an emphasis on the constitutive importance of observations and knowledge to an idealist emphasis on the importance of political, cultural, and ideational factors, which are then studied through a method that abstracts precisely from the observer effect (e.g., Abdelal et al. 2009).

The idea of the constructed nature of identities and institutions has been pursued with rather greater conviction in relatively new fields of study such as cultural economy and social studies of finance (Mackenzie 2006; Callon et al. 2007; Aitken 2007; Langley 2008), where the theme of performativity has aimed at a more radical break with foundationalist assumptions. The concept of performativity serves both as a means to underscore the contingent, constructed character of institutions and identities, and as a means to understand how they achieve whatever degree of coherence they enjoy. The dependence on iterative enactment makes entities inherently fragile, but it also introduces a ritualistic element into the dynamics of their constitution. The central ambition of performativity scholarship has thus been to move beyond a traditional epistemological problematic, and to think of relations, measures, and forms as immanent yet productive; they are performative both in the sense that they need to be performed (have no independent existence) and in the sense that they do something (they alter something in the existing state of affairs). Here the notion of performativity has become closely allied with the theory of speech acts, which states that utterances can sometimes bring about their own truth conditions (as in "I hereby promise") and so highlights the constructive aspects of discourse and language.

Although this is a promising starting point, the performativity problematic as it has found its way into the critical finance literature has mostly mirrored rather than accounted for the paradoxical character of performatives. There is a marked conceptual gap between performativity as a means to highlight the contingent nature of social facts and human institutions, on the one hand, and analyses of the constitutive powers of performativity, on the other. It is often precisely the history, context, or microlevel operation of the felicitous speech act that is insufficiently specified—meaning that the normative force of the speech act is not so much accounted for but instead relied upon as an explanation (Butler 2010). Put differently, the understanding of ordering that is advanced in the performativity problematic still revolves around how it effectively overcomes contingency, rather than how it puts contingency to productive use or stabilizes it from within. Contingency is what makes things dependent on performance, but when it comes to theorizing the constitutive powers of performance, it features less as a dynamic principle than as something to be conquered; contingency introduces the possibility of the failure of a performance, but it is not clear how it is itself a constitutive dimension of successful performances. It is not seen primarily as an active force, but rather as something that might upstage the felicitous transformation of fictions into facts.

Particularly interesting here is the way actor-network theory has moved from its original province—social studies of science—into the study of money and finance. Founded on a definite anti-Kantianism, actor-network theory is highly suspicious of traditional notions of representation, the idea that symbols can stand for something else. As Latour put it, citing his own earliest intuition on this matter: "Nothing can be reduced to anything else, nothing can be deduced from anything else, everything may be allied to everything else" (1988: 163). Entities are plastic: no external set of principles regulates the patterning of associations,

and the logic whereby association generates identities is a fully endogenous one. Actor-network theory thus emphasizes the material logistics
of signification; questions of meaning and reference are viewed in terms
of the topological dynamics of networks. In this way, it seeks to take the
magic out of meaning and signification. Along such lines, actor-network
theory has tended to think of itself as a "material semiotics" (Law 2009:
142) or as "an empirical version of poststructuralism" (145), which un-
derscores the general principle that there is no ontological gap between
things and their representation, or between matter and meaning. Ordering is to be studied as a material process of patterning that follows
a logic of punctualization (Law 1992; Callon 1991), whereby dynamics
of association come to revolve around a particular point and so become
organized into a functional unity—an actant that can itself become an
element in a network of relations. The logic of punctualization is conceived in topological terms; it is the most densely connected element
in the network and so comes to serve as an "obligatory passage point"
(Callon 1986: 205).

For Latour, training our focus on the constructive role of associations and mediations is the only way to avoid a sterile choice between
a naïve realism and an equally naïve idealism. That is, when we are not
mindful of the constructive role of associations, we will end up

> searching for something to fill the void we have created, looking for
> some adequatio, some resemblance between two ontological varieties
> that we have made as dissimilar as possible. It is hardly surprising that
> philosophers have been unable to reach an understanding on the ques-
> tion of realism and relativism: they have taken the two provisional ex-
> tremities for the entire chain, as if they had tried to understand how a
> lamp and a switch could "correspond" to each other after cutting the
> wire and making the lamp "gaze out at the 'external' switch." (1999: 73)

Forgetting forms, mediations, and relations prepares the ground for the
"salto mortale" (74, quoting William James), the leap from the material

actuality of things to an idealism of symbols and language. For Latour this salto mortale is what defines the Kantian reorientation of modern philosophy, an "extravagant form of constructivism" (5) according to which "the outside world now turns around the mind-in-the-vat, which dictates most of that world's laws, laws it has extracted from itself without help from anyone else" (6).

Yet as actor-network theorists have moved into the study of finance, they have found it very difficult not to rely on the very Kantian leap that Latour ridicules so effectively. This has been especially apparent in Callon's prominent work (1998, 2007), which has evolved from a material semiotics to an idealist framework that views economic logics as effects of cognitive frameworks, epistemic devices, and economic theories. Performativity scholarship has at times been prone to a "hagiography of knowledge" (Bryan et al. 2012: 307; cf. Esposito 2013), displaying an exaggerated fascination with the technicalities of practitioner knowledge and a very limited ability to rethink core economic concepts. How might we explain these curious shifts in intellectual affiliations? The somewhat hapless way the ideational dimension is brought back suggests that it was never properly accounted for in the basic framework of actor-network theory—that semiotics was never convincingly integrated into materialism without leaving a remainder, that the poststructuralist dimension was never convincingly rendered intelligible in empirical terms.

If actor-network theory's initial reluctance to engage with imaginaries and fictions was motivated by a healthy concern to avoid traditional metaphysics and representational idealism, its own receptiveness to Kantian idealism suggests it never dealt satisfactorily with this problem. A hostility to traditional metaphysics all too readily morphed into a somewhat dismissive attitude toward questions of observation and reflexivity. Here we might have cause to think that Latour's dismissal of Kantian idealism is a little facile. Although his characterization of Kant's salto mortale is apposite, it is equally important to appreciate why the Kantian response to the break with premodern metaphysics is such a recurrent one. Reading Latour, one almost gets the impression that the problem Kant struggled with—Now that we are no longer able to rely on theological certainties, what can we still expect or hope to know?—was never a real problem to begin with. But questions regarding the status and role of human knowledge are not so easily displaced. The question remains how we should deal with the ability of a configuration to reflect on itself, the paradoxical moment when a pattern takes exception to itself and becomes capable of relating to itself, as if it were not simply itself but more than itself. The "irreductionist" project seeks a clean solution to the problem of the epistemic moment, and this can plausibly be seen as its own kind of reductionism. Paradoxes that are cavalierly sidelined have a way of making themselves felt in unexpected ways and at inconvenient times, and actor-network theory has been prone to get caught in a somewhat unstable back-and-forth between materialism and idealism. It has tended to perform the Kantian leap that it ridicules.

Key here is how the notion of association occupies an absolutely central position in actor-network theory and yet remains itself undertheorized. Taken by itself, the emphasis on the nonrepresentational character of associations does little to account for the particular patterns of clustering they exhibit. Thinking of the punctum as simply a privileged material element in a network does not do much to explain the force at work that marshals the other elements in the network around it. From a Luhmannian (1995) perspective, to say that social constitution occurs through the creation of associations is to beg the question as to the stuff these connections are made of and what propels the dynamics of their patterning (cf. Tellmann et al. 2012: 212). We can only understand the ability of a network to achieve functional coherence if we can theorize the orientation or dispositif that pervades the logistics of association (Appadurai 2011: 536). For Luhmann, the observational moment is central in this regard: the semiotics of association are at their core specular and interactive, driven by continuous mutual observation, anticipation, and projection. It is by virtue of an associative logic of speculative investment, whereby constituent elements come to perceive their own prospects of security as best served by performing certain functions in a wider pattern, that an assemblage achieves a degree of functional coherence and identity. The punctum binds elements into an operational whole by organizing a temporal imaginary, a rationality of memory and expectation that works as an affective force field (Luhmann 1976). In short, what is missing in actor-network theory is a sustained reflection on the ghost in the machine (cf. Appadurai 2011; Farias 2014).

CHAPTER 3

Luhmannian Considerations

For Luhmann, there is no way to truly know whether the nature of things is essentially mind or matter. Any attempt to "solve" the question through a particular theoretical formulation is likely to simply end up in an unstable back-and-forth between materialism and idealism, reifying each in turn and so reproducing rather than productively engaging the paradoxical character of the problem. The ability of a system to relate to itself is an inescapably paradoxical affair: reflexivity is the continuous breaching of the bounds of immanence without ever attaining a transcendental position. The recognition of this is what makes Luhmann's brand of constructivism "radical"; the process through which an identity is assembled never generates a kind of consciousness that can comprehend itself in a transparent manner and know itself objectively. Because the virtual dimension is generated by the interaction between the actual and the inactual (Esposito 2011: 20)—that is, it arises when an entity becomes reflexive and aware of its own historical contingency, able to produce a reading of its past and to make projections—we cannot hope to clarify its role by reducing it to either one or the other. A Luhmannian problematic thus starts from an acknowledgment that traditional problematics of realism and idealism cannot be resolved on their own terms—that whatever side we take on such issues, we will always be left with a remainder, a part of our experience that is not accounted for. It instead treats the paradoxical character of self-reference as a clue to how systems are constructed and operate (Luhmann 1995; Esposito 1996), allowing for the consideration of the virtual dimension from a pragmatic angle that neither essentializes nor trivializes it.

At its most basic level, self-referential observation involves simply the ability of a system to draw a distinction between itself and its environment (Luhmann 1995: 17, 2013: 44), the mere ability to observe itself as contingent, as a constructed configuration of functional connections. Reflexivity is the ability of a system to understand itself as possible but not necessary, actual and therefore potentially inactual—it is at its core a process of temporalization (Luhmann 1995: 310, 2013: 143). Luhmann rejects the (Parsonian) idea that systems can ever operate according to an externally given set of norms or principles. Drawing specifically on second-order systems theory (e.g., Maturana and Varela 1992), he is centrally concerned with the question of how system cohesion emerges endogenously, from within the dynamic of observers observing other observers and the particular feedback loops that come to mark that process (Esposito 2011: 104). Any system observes itself and the boundaries with its environment, but this never flips over into the possibility of external observation or a totalizing point of view. Explanations of order thus cannot be modeled on the idea of an engineer who observes the system from the outside and can make sovereign interventions. If self-organizing processes can evolve strong powers of cohesion and integrative capacities, they only ever work by virtue of the recursive activation of the connections they are composed of; they never transcend this performative condition and never come to be characterized by an objectivity conceived on the idea of substance, an essential identity that subsists of its own accord.

Like the performativity concept, Luhmann's notion of self-reference is marked by a certain duality. In its minimal sense, it denotes "mere" self-referentiality, the ability of a system to recognize itself as a complex assemblage of contingent connections and to become aware of its dependence on the ongoing enactment of that relational configuration. In its maximal sense, self-referentiality denotes the way systems reproduce themselves through their own operations; that is, the emergence of "autopoietic" capacities (Luhmann 2013: 77). But whereas performativity scholarship tends toward a strong disconnect between its minimal and maximal senses (performativity understood as a condition of contingency on the one hand, and as an operation that overcomes contingency on the other), this is not the case with Luhmann's idea of self-reference. The system's recognition and engagement of contingency always remains the driving force of dynamics of self-organization and social construction. A system's Gödelian inability to transcend its own premises and its Münchhausen-like ability to set itself in motion are different sides of the same self-referential coin.

Luhmann's understanding of operational closure needs to be distinguished from the idea of ontological closure (Borch 2011: 23–24). Systems are self-referential not in the sense of being self-sufficient or autonomous but in the sense of having no outside foundation. We should not understand operational closure in the way we imagine inanimate objects being separate from each other, nor in the way we imagine godlike entities to be able to exist without need for external interactions. Systems never transcend contingency and never come to subsist in independence from the outside world, beyond the need for ongoing interaction with their environment (cf. Cilliers 2001: 140–41). The differentiation of system and environment is the precondition for the interactions between them: "in the self-referential mode of operation, closure is a form of broadening possible environmental contacts" (Luhmann 1995: 37). Self-reference is never an expression of ontological self-sufficiency, disconnect, or metaphysical autonomy—it is the mode of constitution in a world where divine acts of creation do not occur and we cannot hope to find essential substances that exist independently of the functional needs of biological or social systems. Indeed, the very operations through which a system achieves autopoietic cohesion simultaneously create sources of contingency that are not functionally incorporated into its field of operations. Stasis is not metaphysical autonomy but means the end of life—death.

Luhmann is most productively read as advancing an understanding of the logic of association—of the way entities become connected to other entities to form new functionally coherent systems—that is more precise than what actor-network theory offers. A system registers the emergence of challenges, threats, disturbances, and vulnerabilities (what Luhmann calls "irritations"), and even just maintaining its existing identity requires that it adjust the configuration of operational connections that compose it, which involves establishing connections with other elements and rearranging boundaries. A system is always under pressure to do something, to select from among the myriad connections possible (Luhmann 2002b: 160). Incapable of transcending its own point of view and unable to get an objective perspective on what it needs, it must speculate, make decisions without having all relevant knowledge.

At its root, the speculative character of life derives from the fact that the act of observation cannot observe itself. The classic image here is that of the eye that cannot see itself, and the constitutive blind spot this indicates is central to Luhmann's work (Luhmann 2013: 103, 114; Moeller 2006: 73). A system's machinery of seeing can be extremely sophisticated, but it cannot observe the totality of its own operations in real time and it cannot therefore ever fully predict or comprehensively control the effects of its own functioning. System reproduction always generates novelty and complexity that the system cannot anticipate or symbolize through those very capacities (Luhmann 2013: 105). Every act of self-referential reproduction is therefore speculative, beset by an irreducible element of uncertainty that cannot be neutralized as a matter of principle. Crucially, however, it's not just that my relationship to the world is characterized by uncertainty; it's also that the world, made up of other systems, responds to this fact; which is something that I know and must also respond to. The world is composed of observers who observe other observers, and our speculations constantly need to adjust as they size up and locate a moving target: "Speculation takes its cue from speculation" (Luhmann 2002a: 185). This dynamic, which Luhmann terms "double contingency" and corresponds closely to the economic logic of specularity (Orléan 1989) that we introduced earlier, entails a rapid multiplication of sources of contingency. The world is not just contingent, but often highly volatile.

The dynamics of specularity are stabilized not by external norms or principles but endogenously, through the way mutual expectations form to produce a new, higher-level systemic logic (Luhmann 1995: 303). The operative dynamic here is neither material assimilation nor conceptual definition but synchronization ("firing together"). To create a pattern of mutual expectations means to establish a resonance that allows elements to operate in tandem, thereby creating a more or less stable connection between entities that can itself function as a system. Anticipations, particular orientations toward the future that make uncertainty manageable, are the "stuff" of which social relations are made. The semiotics of association are temporal in nature—driven by continuous mutual anticipation and projection. A pattern of connections that is formed in this way never becomes nonperformative: a system remains forever dependent on the recursive activation of the patterns through which it has emerged (Clam 2000: 66; Borch 2011: 28). A systemic dynamic therefore never escapes volatility, an insight that is well expressed in Shackle's understanding of the "kaleidic" nature of expectations: "Like the symmetric pattern of colours in the kaleidoscope, [expectations] can be changed comprehensively and radically by a slight shock or twist given to the instrument, or to the evidence in the mind of the expectation-former" (1972: 183).

In some respects Luhmann's understanding of how entities associate to create networks characterized by their own identity and coherence runs parallel to the way actor-network theory depicts this process. But in his emphasis on observation, specularity, and temporalization we nonetheless find an important difference, one that provides a significant critical edge. In actor-network theory, contingency features primarily

as an ontological qualification, a factor that prevents objects from enjoying the purity that moderns have imagined for them. In Luhmann's
thought, contingency is a more dynamic factor that at all times drives
the process of constitution and opens up a much wider range of concerns about the role of risk and not-knowing in the constitution of
social life. Uncertainty, ignorance, and the need to make speculative
decisions are driving forces behind the construction of identities. Although for Luhmann systems are defined by their capacity for observation, he always considers this in conjunction with the limitations of
that epistemic function and the active role those limitations play in the
construction of human life.

Actors know that other actors face epistemic limitations similar in
nature to the ones they are facing themselves, and this becomes something they strategize around. In the logic of double contingency, the
outcome of our investments is to a large extent determined by the investments they induce, and so it is often much more important to be
known in this or that way than to expand one's knowledge. Control in a
risk society depends on *being known* in a context of pervasive uncertainty,
the ability to serve as a central point of reference in the specular logic of
contingent claims, as an attractor for others' speculative investments. In
this context, the purposeful creation of uncertainty and insecurity can
even be a source of advantage, allowing actors to shore up their normative position. It is this modality of endogenous hierarchization that I
have sought to capture with the concept of leverage, a mode of ordering
that works not by eliminating uncertainty but by capitalizing on it. A
system is in many ways an "ecology of ignorance" (Luhmann 1998: 75;
cf. Esposito 2011: 14).[1]

The creation of a new systemic dynamic is possible because leveraging plays on the uncertainty that existing systems experience as they
move into the future. At work here is a particular interaction of memory
and expectation. Any actor has access to an infrastructure of practical
reason, a network of investments and associations that can be taken
for granted and readily relied upon (Cilliers 1998: 92). Such a system

of implicit memory allows us to organize our relation to the future; it allows us to generate expectations and to think probabilistically (Luhmann 1995: 41). Without memory, an actor is rudderless, bound to become lost in the dynamics of unconstrained specularity and disoriented "in an infinite game of cross-references with no holds, handles or limits" (Esposito 2011: 26). The past "serves as a means of selection" (26). In other words, expectation is always based on a system's relationship to its past, which permits the formation of habits (Human 2015: 54). But of course, we often find that a cluster of routines and expectations we adopted turns out to have much less functional value than we earlier hoped or imagined it would. And this awareness rarely automatically translates into an ability to generate a new reading of our history. The fact that our ability to perceive problems always exceeds the ability to diagnose them stems from the fact that we cannot easily separate ourselves from the problem: our reflexive capacities are not available without activating the chains of connections through which they have been constituted. We can't go "off-line," step out of ourselves to examine the mechanisms of our functioning from an outside perspective and isolate the malfunctioning parts.

If contingency were simply an external condition, we would be absolved of responsibility. But since we know that our speculations are an active force in shaping the future, we experience an anxious pressure to make a decision while having insufficient knowledge (Massumi 2014: 9). Under conditions of intensifying uncertainty, the hierarchizing logic of risk becomes more pronounced: actors tend to refrain from experimentation and resort to tried-and-tested patterns. It is not that in such situations of uncertainty they become paralyzed, simply "defaulting" into compliance with existing norms. The recourse to norms is not so much a way of abandoning decision but rather a way of keeping options open, of ensuring that we live to fight another day—reflexive powers may be available and alert, and precisely for that reason be disposed to postpone making major decisions. We can improve our own prospects of persistence by associating ourselves with a larger, more powerful entity,

even if in the process we increase its leverage over us. Often the most
feasible way for a system to adapt to the challenges it faces and achieve
a degree of security is to elaborate its connections to a wider systemic
dynamic. As risk becomes incalculable, the weight of the past appears as
the promise of the future.

Viewing association through the lens of leveraging provides a critical twist—it is a way to move beyond the tendency in social and political
theory to think of association in overly egalitarian or politically neutral
terms. This tendency is pronounced in actor-network theory, but more
generally has deep roots in related modes of thought such as Deweyan
pragmatism, Tocquevillian notions of civic association, and pluralism
in the Fabian tradition. Whereas for Latour contingency becomes the
rationale for what amounts to an ontological pluralism, from a Luhmannian perspective such pluralism is just as problematic as a metaphysical monism or any other position that prejudges the dynamics of
self-organization. The formation of a system never eradicates uncertainty and the need to speculate—it addresses some of the risks faced by
the lower-level entities that compose it, but at the same time it generates new ones. The emergence of a new, higher-level system amounts
to the installation of a new capacity for self-reference that faces its own
outside and is unable to assess its problems from an objective, external
point of view. It is precisely the way systems continuously produce new
sources of contingency that creates a permanent pressure for hierarchization, a permanent pressure for systems to seek out alliances and
integrate themselves into higher-level systems.

CHAPTER 4

System, Economy, and Governance

Autopoietic capacities become more effective in higher-level systems built on a large number of subsystems. Complex systems have emerged through many iterations of hierarchization and enjoy a degree of resilience, a heightened ability to adapt to and absorb challenges. Self-reference in its maximal sense (that is, autopoiesis) is a paradoxical phenomenon: it involves the presence of strong internal cohesion and an unmistakable unity of identity in the absence of any discernable underlying substance or objective ontological ground (cf. Luhmann 1995: 41). No amount of analysis will lead us to the foundations of the edifice; we are continuously referred to new promises, anticipations, projections, and expectations, yet never find what is promised. To say that present-day money is a fully plastic entity is to claim that it manifests these paradoxical dynamics to an extremely high degree. Defining money positively is impossible: we can only analyze it as a circular movement of deferrals, speculative investments driven precisely by the absence of foundational certainties, hedges on the impossibility of knowing with certainty how our interactions are shaping the future. As a self-referential entity, money is both pure fiction and pure fact, incarnating its own significance. Money is an entirely virtual moment that enjoys no independent existence yet exerts a powerful organizing effect on the very patterns through which it is produced.

This is of course the sense in which money is often referred to as a secular god. As Simmel (2011 [1900]: 254) points out, money manifests the "coincidentia oppositorum" that often served as the theological definition of divinity. Although this can be a useful way to frame the paradoxical nature of economy, we nonetheless need to tread cautiously here, as it is not uncommon to take this paradox not as an entry point for the critical interrogation of money but instead as itself a template for social-scientific explanation. This is readily apparent in Agamben's economic theology (2011), but it can also be observed in other approaches that, while less overtly indebted to traditional theological themes, tend to reproduce the paradoxical manifestations of self-referentiality (e.g., Taylor 2008; Ayache 2010). Serres's conception of the joker suggests a more pragmatic take on money's paradoxical character as a coincidence of opposites. By performatively demonstrating the non-necessary character of existing functions and values, the joker comes to command a privileged capacity for producing new connections and new futures. Money, "the most joker of jokers" (1982: 161), is a way for a system to symbolize its own limitations and to do something productive with the impossibility of surpassing contingency or manipulating it with foresight. A similar logic characterizes Rotman's understanding of modern money, which he develops in analogy with the role of the number zero: by marking absence, it gives that absence a certain symbolic presence (1987: 13). The ability to signify the impossibility of external, neutral observation is what Rotman sees as the crucial innovation of modernity.

Money is a way to do something constructive with our inability to transcend or eradicate contingency; it allows us to "operationalize our lack of knowledge" (Esposito 2011: 51). It provides a symbolic marker for the impossibility of transcending uncertainty, and in this paradoxical capacity it makes a productive intervention into the semiotics of human life. Money enters our world only when our knowledge of that world becomes limited. It is a vanishing point, a point that marks groundlessness and the ineradicability of contingency, and in that capacity it provides the interaction of speculative investments with a point of reference. Through its ability to signify the impossibility of nonspeculative signification, it becomes the closest thing that we have to security. As much as we may be aware of its symbolic character, money functions as one of the most unambiguous norms and predictable sources of control that we have in modern life, a uniquely objective fact, the social institution that we have least reason to question. Money's character as a coincidence of opposites therefore expresses itself most pointedly in a temporal register: if we could predict the future, money would be without value; but given conditions of uncertainty, money holds out the promise of a secure future. Money is indefinite: both fully contingent and of potentially unlimited duration. Capitalist temporality thus works on an affectively charged tension between the acute awareness of ineradicable contingency on the one hand, and the anticipation of riskless security and infinite time on the other (Konings 2015).

Despite his at times almost gleeful interest in paradoxes, Luhmann never quite appreciated the depth of the paradox that is posed by money and the unique ordering capacity that it expresses; his conception of money was fairly conventional, focused on its exchange function (Deutschmann 1999: 72). Luhmann understood religion and ideology as separate subsystems of society, which makes it difficult to view those dimensions as receiving concentrated expressions in economic life. As much as his analyses of self-reference work as arguments against any tendency to prejudge the dynamics of system formation, he never reconsidered the classic sociological schema of society as organized through different (economic, legal, political, cultural, etc.) subsystems (Thornhill 2006; Borch 2011). Although he was aware that systems never transcend the need for ongoing interactions with their environment, his theorization of the way their relation becomes stabilized nonetheless often assumed a durable "structural coupling," suggesting that a system can achieve a coupling to an environment in a way that does not itself entail the creation of new systemness. On such a reading, the process of system formation stabilizes enough to bring that very process to a halt, and the environment comes to feature primarily as the source of inputs and the recipient of outputs. At times overly concerned with the interaction of discretely differentiated systems, his analysis of the dynamics of hierarchization was somewhat abortive. In particular, Luhmann's work fails to acknowledge that one of the defining characteristics of contemporary life is the erosion of boundaries between the economy and other spheres, "the waning of functional differentiation" (Vogl 2015: 100; cf. Arvidsson 2011; Lazzarato 2012). Money, seen from a properly antifoundational understanding of ordering (which would reject the idea of an inherent gap between economic value and the normative capacities of cultural and political discourses), is not simply a medium of a particular subsystem, but a norm with a totalizing reach, characterized by a degree of self-referentiality and ordering capacity that other norms are not (Deutschmann 2011: 91).

Ironically, Luhmann's systems theory offers little insight into one of the most significant systemic developments of our time, namely the expansion and growing reach of financial processes and the ways they penetrate into structures that in earlier times were characterized by a degree of independence. His work never meaningfully registers the fact that one of its central organizing concepts—self-referentiality—receives an extremely pronounced manifestation in the self-expansion and self-valorization of financial capital. Thus, instead of following Luhmann's work on what he conceived of as the economic subsystem (e.g., 1988), we are better off taking those elements of his general social theory discussed in the previous chapter as a useful set of reflections on the problematic of economy properly understood. Of course, to argue that the problematic of economy consists in the question of how order arises out of uncertainty is to be out of step with prevailing definitions: orthodox economics addresses the issue of scarcity, with all problems besetting this question reduced to technical puzzles about the logistics of provisioning, while sidestepping more challenging questions by reducing uncertainty to calculable risk. But the reformulation suggested here is not an arbitrary one: even a somewhat cursory genealogy of the concept of economy will be able to situate questions of knowledge and uncertainty as constitutive aspects of the problematic of economy.

In premodern times, the concept of economy was overtly religious and political: it referred to the orientations and dispositions that ensured that human practices would reproduce the divinely ordained order of things (Cameron 2008; Düppe 2011). Economy was God's means of ensuring the transformation of earthly indeterminacy into the submission to divine principles, and so to ward off the pernicious effects of secular contingency. Some of the activities that we nowadays think of as specifically economic in nature (such as financial speculation and moneylending) were viewed as chrematistical forces that precisely had a corrosive effect on the maintenance of economic order. It is only around the time of Adam Smith that the concept of economy took on a more secular meaning. In the context of the Scottish Enlightenment, when it became increasingly difficult to believe literally that human history was orchestrated by an outside force, the mechanisms whereby contingency is transformed into order were increasingly viewed as situated at the level of the secular itself, as related to the ways human actors practically handle the uncertainties generated by their interactions. What became thinkable was the idea of secular self-organization, as expressed in Smith's notion of the "invisible hand": mechanisms of coordination were increasingly seen as immanent to mundane human activities (Hamowy 1987; Horwitz 2001; Sheehan and Wahrman 2015). In this context, activities centered on money-dealing acquired a degree of legitimacy they had hitherto lacked. Through the workings of the invisible hand, such practices could advance order, supporting rather than undermining economic governance. Smith's work on the social division of labor and the role of the market amounted to an argument that the speculative engagement of the future, acting under conditions of uncertainty and without divine guarantees, could under certain conditions be legitimate.

This of course represents a rather different take on Smith than the one we are likely to be familiar with, but it does not necessarily mean

that contemporary mainstream economics is mistaken in considering
Smith to be its founder. After all, Smith was also one of the first to
formulate the idea of the neutrality of the market, the idea that money
was a mere device that allowed to take place more efficiently a set of
exchanges already inherent in the structure of a barter economy. At
the same time as money was grasped as having specific coordinating
functions, doing a job that previously had been God's (the governance
of contingency), it came to be seen as principally neutral. Smith advanced *both* an intuition of the idea of secular self-organization *and* the
core fantasy that has always attended that process. In this way, Smith's
thought manifested the constitutive duality in the way moderns think
about economy, simultaneously asserting the contingency of the future
and the possibility of objectively discounting this future. Together with
the emerging legitimacy of secular time arises the idea that time can be
neutralized. We will later examine the significance of this paradoxical
double movement; here the point is simply to note its existence, and to
note that orthodox economic theory has tended to suppress and sanitize
this paradoxical logic.

This suppression has of course never been fully effective. Mainstream economics itself has engaged in considerable detail with the
problem of information and its imperfections, although it continues to
see these as deviations from a market characterized by equilibrium. Heterodox traditions have always been highly critical of the cavalier treatment of information and knowledge in mainstream economic thought.
Post-Keynesian theory in particular has argued that orthodoxy's exclu-
sive focus on quantifiable risk ignores the importance of real, incalculable uncertainty. But to separate uncertainty from calculable risk in this
way is itself problematic. Such an approach still relies on an understanding of probability as positive knowledge about the future rather than
as a means to handle our lack of such knowledge (Esposito 2007), and
uncertainty features as an external limit to statistical probability rather
than as something that is always already at play in the engagement
of risk (Kessler 2009; Appadurai 2015). We may recall here Keynes's

famous comment about value being like a beauty contest, which drives at a notion of specularity. Although this has had a significant impact on the development of post-Keynesian work, it is almost always referred to in support of arguments that contrast the self-referentiality and groundlessness of speculative finance with the rational kind of finance that serves the production of real value. Shackle holds Keynes himself as at least partly responsible for the way his work has been appropriated in both mainstream and post-Keynesian theory: while on the one hand his formulations in the *General Theory* suggest a positivist approach to risk and probability (Shackle 1972: xviii),[1] on the other hand "he had, essentially, only one thing to say about expectation: that it eludes reduction to clear and stable principles and laws" (180). As Butos and Koppl put it, "Keynes was a Cartesian rationalist who saw about him a non-Cartesian social world" (1997: 349). Genuine uncertainty is thus taken to indicate the point at which economic action becomes irrational, driven by speculations rather than real value.

The upshot has been an inability to systematically foreground the problematic of economy as the question of how order arises out of contingency. The heterodox critique of mainstream notions of equilibrium and efficient markets revolves around the idea that speculation is a disordering impulse that undermines coherent governance, and in this way it returns to a premodern critique of chrematistics. Often focused too singularly on a rejection of the notion that markets can be self-regulating, post-Keynesian and other heterodox perspectives are unable to relate productively to Smith's identification of a secular economy, a logic of financial interaction that is characterized by certain self-organizing mechanisms and thereby functions as a modality of governance. Although we should certainly appreciate that the way mainstream economics has formulated Smith's argument (that is, in the language of equilibrium and efficient markets) is highly problematic, that should not lead us to sideline the issue altogether. Whereas mainstream economics sanitizes Smith's invisible hand and turns it into a detemporalized notion of equilibrium, heterodox theories largely dismiss this question of economy as

self-organization. Such considerations are especially important in understanding the contemporary era, which is characterized by the expansion
of economic and financial rationalities and their penetration into hitherto separate spheres. Critical approaches have tended to consider this in
terms of the changing interactions between different subsystems, viewing it as a process whereby capacities for governance become constrained
and weakened ("colonized"). In this way, they have given relatively little
consideration to the new modalities of governance these same processes
open up. The internalization of economic rationalities into logics of politics and governance produces its own ordering mechanisms, even though
those resemble neither traditional models of sovereign power nor the
styles of consensus and legitimacy production that we tend to associate
with the rise of twentieth-century political democracy (Brown 2003).

Contemporary transformations of governance are fruitfully exam-
ined through a systems-theoretical lens.[2] A system's performative and
recursive nature means that even though it can register irritations and
perceive the malfunctioning of key functions, it does not have access to
an off-line self-repair function. As a consequence, reform and adjustment have a notoriously bootstrap-like character: the changes that a system needs to make appear to be the preconditions for making them. As
suggested in the Introduction, and as we will see at greater length in
subsequent chapters, this is a useful vantage point from which to understand the contradictions that beset financial governance during the
1970s, which had everything to do with the way political and regulatory
institutions had become imbricated with dynamics of financial expansion. And whereas progressively inclined perspectives have generally
continued to assume that prospects for coherent governance depend on
the possibility of public institutions extricating themselves from speculative financial processes, a key strength of the neoliberal project has been
to recognize the limits of such rationalist approaches and to discern the
possibilities for steering and ordering opened up by the ways politics and
governance are increasingly endogenous to the logic of economy.

CHAPTER 5

Foucault beyond the Critique of Economism

The previous chapter suggested a conception of economy as a process of ordering through uncertainty, and it criticized Luhmann for artificially separating this from other spheres of social life and so limiting the province of economic principles somewhat arbitrarily. In other words, I have argued that Luhmann did not seize the opportunity afforded by his work to formulate—what we might term—a "non-essentialist economism." The latter concept will to many seem a contradiction in terms. But we have seen the profound problems that attach to existing critiques of economism, and the way they themselves invoke foundational values. Here I would like to develop a perspective that takes economy as the central ordering mechanism of modern society without succumbing to the problems of essentialism and determinism. To this end, the present chapter will enlist a somewhat unlikely ally—Foucault, long known as one of the main critics of economism. Challenging the idea of economic materialism from a more committed antifoundational perspective, Foucauldian poststructuralism always offered a more thoughtful critique of economism than the new pluralism did. But the fact that even this was never particularly satisfying as an intellectual appropriation has been hinted at by the interest triggered in recent years by Foucault's later

work, where he draws close connections among the expansion of capitalism, the logic of risk, and the changing nature of governance.

We should situate this turn properly in its intellectual context. For
a long time, Foucault's work had a dual status as both a critique of economic determinism and a critique of power conceived on the model of
sovereignty. That is, on the one hand, it was widely viewed as rejecting the Marxist interpretation of the development of modern capitalism
as driven by material and technological forces, insisting instead on the
constitutive role of knowledge, discourse, and representation. On the
other hand, Foucault's work was an argument for the displacement of
sovereign power by the disciplinary effects of discursive norms and epistemic techniques, and a critique of theoretical perspectives that reproduced the illusions of sovereignty. Along such lines, some of the most
influential appropriations of Foucault (Dean 1999; Miller and Rose
2008) positioned him above all as a theorist of disciplinary governance
and so tended to dissolve questions of both politics and economics into
a sociological soup of internalized norms and values. We encounter
here a strongly Kantian Foucauldianism (Braidotti 2007), which views
contemporary subjectivity in terms of its responsiveness to risk-based
norms and calculative rationalities.

The most prominent and relevant (at least for our purposes) philosophical challenge to such perspectives was formulated in Agamben's
(1998, 2005) work, which takes issue with the tendency to overestimate
the internal cohesion of disciplinary governance and rejects the argument that sovereignty has been absorbed or displaced by discipline.
Agamben views sovereignty as rooted in the state's ability to except itself
from society's basic normative order when an emergency situation presents itself. He depicts the constitution of order not as a smooth process
of knowledge-based integration but as an ongoing logic of emergency
and exception. It is the element of incalculable risk that is seen to occasion the sovereign decision. This theoretical template is of interest not
just in its own right, but also because it provides a rigorous formulation
of the conceptual structure that underlies the more general assumption

that neoliberalism is not grounded in a normative order and that its reproduction is dependent on exceptional measures. Such approaches view both the rise and the reproduction of neoliberalism as heavily dependent on the exceptional institutional machinations of neoliberal elites, their ability to use state institutions in a way that allows them to bypass the organic production of consent and legitimacy.

The depiction of the sovereign decision as transcending the ordinary logic of risk gives Agamben's work an essentializing thrust: he depicts the power of exception as an ability to step out of the temporal logic of speculative claims, sovereignty as effectively working outside, before or beyond, risk. There has been no shortage of compelling critiques of Agamben's conception of the role of the state in terms of its ability to suspend normality and to operate directly on the vacated territory of bare life (e.g., Johns 2005; Buck-Morss 2007; Huysmans 2008; Neocleous 2008). Consequently, even as the notion of exception has become widely used in the critical analysis of neoliberal politics, this has nonetheless been accompanied by a certain distancing from Agamben's dramatic depictions of sovereign decisionism and the blanket suspension of law. Agamben's conceptual schema has been largely appropriated in a "pluralized" form that depicts neoliberal sovereignty as a complex construction of competing claims to exceptional status (Connolly 2005; Ong 2006; Honig 2009; Amoore 2013; Adey et al. 2015).

But we may wonder if this really settles the issue convincingly. On the one hand, such perspectives still understand neoliberal authority as bypassing a more basic normative structure needed for consent and legitimation. On the other hand, something important might be lost with the dilution of Agamben's uncompromising insistence on the salience of sovereignty. To reject the idea that acts of authorization ever align themselves to produce authority structures that are sovereign in the distinctive sense of that word—that is, unconditional and nonnegotiable—would seem to turn a blind eye to the form that state agency often does take in contemporary capitalism. If it is one thing to emphasize that the exception never achieves the nondiscursive, real, or ontological force that it claims, taking this as a rationale for a return to a pluralist conception of authority seems all too convenient. For instance, such a perspective does not allow us to say much about the sovereignty the American state deployed in response to the financial crisis, which involved interventions on an extraordinary scale that operated with a high degree of necessity. And this was only the most dramatic manifestation of a dynamic that has been evident throughout the neoliberal era, when sudden crises simply required bailouts, no questions asked. But then again, to follow Agamben by portraying this as a suspension of normal mechanisms of interaction would be to essentialize the state's claim to sovereign status. We should therefore be able to understand the seemingly instantaneous conversion of intense uncertainty into unambiguous authority not as involving a transcendence of risk but precisely in terms of the principles endogenous to it. Crisis entails not the suspension of norms but their unconditional activation.

It may of course well be that Agamben intends his work to be understood along such lines—in which case my point is simply that the conceptual tools he supplies do not give sufficient effect to that intention, and that in the end he simply relies on theology to account for the paradoxes of risk. What is missing is a sustained engagement with the distinctive logic of secular temporality, that is, the economic rationality of continuously needing to make decisions under conditions of uncertainty. Agamben's (2011) recent turn to economic genealogy is certainly interesting in this respect, but it represents above all an attempt to draw questions of economy into the conceptual template of his political theology. Economy is understood in its premodern sense, as the divine capacity to govern by transcending contingency. Notably absent from Agamben's work is any connection to the necessarily speculative character of secular decision, and his book contains no analysis of the way economy took on its distinctive modern connotations. In an important sense, then, Agamben is simply too quick to politicize the paradox of self-reference (Buck-Morss 2007: 171). With Luhmann, we need to appreciate that it is not at all clear how we could conceive a form of life that is not characterized by the paradoxical logic of emergence and exception; therefore, this paradox cannot by itself function as the basis of critique. Whereas Agamben takes the paradigm of self-reference as a way to escape from a problematic of risk, speculation, and contingency, in a Luhmannian perspective they are seen as inextricably intertwined. As a result, Agamben—and more generally the exceptionalist conceptual template that he formalizes—misses a distinctive and highly consequential characteristic of contemporary economic governance, namely neoliberalism's ability to recognize that the state never escapes the secular logic of contingency and risk.

Agamben's work responds specifically to the sidelining of sovereignty in Kantian-Foucauldian scholarship; it has almost nothing to say about the neglect of economics. From this perspective the publication of Foucault's late lectures at the Collège de France has been particularly interesting. They too bring questions of sovereignty back into the picture, but they do so in a way that makes room for their articulation with questions of economy. Sovereignty is here conceptualized as a configuration of "incessant transactions which modify, or move, or drastically change, or insidiously shift sources of finance, modes of investment, decision-making centers, forms and types of control" (2008 [1979]: 77). In this later work, Foucault effects a shift in focus from the role of knowledge in constructing disciplinary regimes to a more open-ended concern with the relationship between order and risk, seen as involving an ineradicable element of uncertainty. Key here is his differentiation of biopolitical normalization from the disciplinary norm (2007 [1978]: 55–57): whereas the latter is associated with a transcendental understanding of power, the former involves a more pragmatic and relational understanding of normativity, seen as an endogenously generated point of reference that exerts organizing effects on the contingent processes from which it is born. Normalization comes to be understood as a process of self-organization, working through the subtle ways in which an ongoing process of contingent association becomes modulated and the resulting assemblages become oriented. The later Foucault thus brings back the speculative dimension of risk in a way that was not really anticipated in the Kantian appropriation of Foucault: the engagement of risk is understood not as representing a norm, but rather in terms of the continuous breaching of existing norms that nonetheless generates its own sources of normativity.[1] It is not that the contemporary subject's orientation to risk becomes itself a coherent norm, but rather that even as its speculative practices continuously transgress existing norms and measures, they engender dynamics characterized by particular patterns of self-organization.

Of course, prior to the publication of Foucault's late lectures, a somewhat related shift had already been seen in his tendency to relativize the efficacy of discipline, over the course of the *History of Sexuality* trilogy (1978–86). But that development could still be—and often was—interpreted as a shift from a structuralist to a postmodern perspective on discourse. Foucault's analysis in the Collège de France lectures goes beyond a postmodern emphasis on indeterminacy to focus on the problematic of government through risk—the distinctive forms of order emerging in a society that is increasingly concerned with the uncertainty of the future (Lemke 2007). The significance of this emphasis has been discerned with acuity by scholars who have noted the convergence of security and political economy problematics in Foucault's late work (Dillon 2008; de Goede 2012; Langley 2013b). If secularized subjectivity is constitutively regulated by a security dispositif (that is, an orientation to safeguarding the integrity of the contingent operational connections that compose it), the self-regulation of this evolving assemblage must occur in real time. Continuous interventions are necessary but they never escape the speculative condition. But even though the modern subject never achieves the security that it imagines, the anticipation of it creates a certain political rationality that itself serves as a binding force. The image of riskless security always serves as a receding horizon, but in that very capacity it nonetheless creates an affective charge that works as the ghost in the machine.

We can see here in Foucault's work a certain convergence with Roberto Esposito's thought, which seeks to move beyond the Kantian-Foucauldian image of disciplinary governance but without reproducing the essentializing valences of Agambenian exceptionalism. Like Luhmann, Esposito emphasizes the impossibility of settling the question of immanence and transcendence, norm and exception. The operation of sovereignty is seen in terms of an "immanent transcendence" (2008: 60); the exception, in Santner's interpretation of Esposito, "marks '*the residue of transcendence that immanence cannot reabsorb*'" (Santner 2011: 21; italics in original). For Esposito, modernity is centrally defined by the productive tension between the ever-present need to engage risk and the prospect of immunity. The modern paradigm of security is situated in the tension between the subject's awareness of its own constructedness and the promise of purity.

Neoliberalism has always intuited the productive force of this tension. The way neoliberalism has brought speculation into the heart of governmental rationality means that it functions on a logic of preemption, a paradoxical practice that fully blurs the distinction between prevention and activation (Massumi 2005, 2007; Cooper 2006; de Goede 2008; Anderson 2010). Preemptive reason is characterized by an awareness of its own speculative foundations and a willingness to move beyond a naïve doctrine of prevention; even as it presents itself as eliminating threats and obstacles to security, its modus operandi and ordering capacity are predicated on the possibility of activating new sources of contingency. The paradoxes of preemptive temporality intensify during times of crisis, when acute uncertainty tends to create its own kind of certainty—precisely not an ability to act on accurate knowledge of the future, but a definite certainty as to what needs to be done in the absence of such knowledge (cf. Tellmann 2009: 18). When emergence becomes emergency, boundless contingency inexplicably coincides with indisputable necessity. At such times, it is perfectly clear what we must do—we have to protect the nodal points of the existing patterns of our temporal interconnectedness, fortify the hubs of the financial system by safeguarding the investments of the banks. During the financial crisis, sovereignty became highly speculative, investing itself in assets whose value was fundamentally in doubt; but at the very same time its policies were grounded in the widespread (if resentful) recognition that it was simply doing what had to be done. An intense concern with the future thus comes to be marked by a strangely reactionary quality. As Massumi puts it: "The before-after seizes the present. The future-past colonizes the present" (2005: 6). Or as Adams, Murphy, and Clarke put it, "the future arrives as already formed in the present, as if the emergency has already happened" (2009: 249). The preemptive temporal rationality engendered by governance through risk now makes itself felt as a foreclosure on the future (cf. Santner 2011: 21).

CHAPTER 6

Time, Investment, and Decision

Bringing time into the analysis is of course a familiar move in the social sciences. Most often, this is in response to dissatisfaction with static and essentializing approaches that assume the reproduction of a given state of affairs. The stress on time along such lines emphasizes change in order to make static analyses more realistic. This is reflected in the well-known distinction between diachronic and synchronic perspectives and the conviction that we need both to understand continuity as well as change. While this move is often useful as a corrective to structuralist perspectives, it is important to appreciate its limitations. It brings time in only insofar as it relates to change, and by projecting time as a source of change onto a foundational world where things subsist autonomously, it maintains a conceptual externality between time and identity. It disarticulates reproduction and change, and it cannot account for self-organizing dynamics as being built in and through time (cf. Baert 1992: 16; Adam 1990). However, emphasizing the binding force of time is not a straightforward move. It is all too easy to jump straight from the emphasis on contingency to an idealist notion of duration. Such a perspective has difficulty accounting for the pragmatic production of time, the way systems temporalize their experience of the world to improve their ability to handle contingency. Social theory should be able to theorize "the specific internal problematic of time—i.e. the constitution of the present through the difference between two time horizons, past and future" (Luhmann 1978: 96). Temporalization is a way to build up memory and expectation and so to intervene productively in the recursive nature of system reproduction. It is a means to create "a freedom of projection and a selectivity of remembrance" (Esposito 2011: 25).

Thinking in terms of past and future is a prominent characteristic of modernity. In the premodern worldview, there was no such thing as a secular temporality, a time specific to life on earth (Luhmann 1976: 130). What characterized secular life was precisely the lack of autonomous time. Just as the premodern subject had only a limited sense of the past as being different from the present, so it did not understand the future as principally open (Hohn 1984: 6)—the future was uncertain only in the sense that humanity could not know what God had in store for the world (Thrift 1990: 108). The future would either look pretty much like today or be something else altogether, an unfathomable state only accessible through divine revelation. For all practical intents and purposes, "the future would have been imagined to be in the same form as the past" (108). A future in the way that modern subjects experience it—as principally open, susceptible to manipulation by our own actions in the present but never fully predictably—was not part of what could be comprehended. The present was not understood as a bridge between past and future, as having emerged out of a historical past and generating a contingent future. Secular time was not understood as capable of internally evolving to become more than a transient present.

The premodern critique of secular temporality was closely associated with the critique of money, which was often formulated as a rejection of money's claim to independent time (Le Goff 1998; Alliez 1996). For Aristotle, money could fulfill a legitimate function when it facilitated exchange that was firmly embedded in a larger cosmic or political order, its purposes defined by those overarching structures (Meikle 1994: 27). This proper, "economic" use of money was to be contrasted with "chrematistics," the concern merely to augment a quantity of money through buying cheap and selling dear, or simply by lending money against interest. Money was seen to engender a linear time that was empty, abstract, without purpose, end, or limit (Vogl 2015: 89). For Aristotle, money pursued for its own sake signified means overtaking ends, an irrational self-referentiality that imagined itself limitless. Christianity allied the critique of chrematistics with the condemnation of idolatry, the attribution of transcendent, self-referential power to secular objects. Money could not multiply or grow itself; it was "sterile" (Düppe 2011: 95). The crime of usurers consisted in dealing in something that was not theirs to trade: time, the duration given by God to the world. The emphasis on temporality makes it comprehensible why theologians did not see any essential difference between such activities as moneylending, hoarding, insurance, and gambling—they all involved attempts to speculate on the future and thus to subvert the economic order instituted by God (Thrift 1990; Le Goff 1998).

The rise of modern capitalism was accompanied by the emergence of a secular experience of time (Koselleck 1981: 170), one in which humanity saw itself as making its own temporality, increasingly understanding present practices as having emerged out of a past and as shaping a contingent future. Humanity recognized itself as making history, as introducing irreversibilities. History came to be thought as "a domain of probability and human prudence" (173), a sphere where human actions and decisions matter in shaping a future that is not already written. Awareness of the past deepened and was no longer limited to the official history of the church; and the sense of the future was no longer polarized between simple repetition of the past and the prospect of end-time salvation. Time was increasingly experienced not simply as an elementary before/after that forever repeats itself, but as a source of variation that means the future is open, its shape not yet determined or known. As Koselleck puts it, "modern time has only been conceived as such since expectations have moved away from all previous experiences" (2002: 128). The particular political rationality that is shaped through this new

relation to time is best expressed in the rise of republicanism, which saw
"[t]he path of history [as leading] away from the tyranny of the past—
toward the republic of the future" (128). Modern republicanism is centrally concerned with the problematic of founding a secure future not on
the imagined divine origins of authority but precisely on the awareness
of contingent origins (Pocock 1975; Allen 2008).

Time now becomes a practical question, something that we need
to handle in particular ways to sustain life and manage contingency:
"time becomes a problem and is not anymore reproduced exclusively
in theological conceptualizations" (Luhmann 1978: 107). Seen from
one angle, the present expands: the present is no longer blunt actuality
but becomes filled with the virtuality of memory and expectations—the
present becomes "specious" (Luhmann 2013: 145). Seen from another
angle, the present contracts: it is a moment of transition between past
and future, a "turning point which switches the process of time from
past into future" (Luhmann 1976: 133), a point-like, evanescent moment of actuality within the virtual flow of time. The present becomes a
moment of decision, where we must confront contingency; it becomes
eventally, experientially stamped by the possibility that something may
happen that cannot easily be reversed (Luhmann 2013: 153; cf. Hohn
1984: 89). Moderns experience the present as a point at which the
transition from past to future is shaped rather than merely being one
point in an externally determined pattern (cf. Shackle 1972: 278–79).
Koselleck notes how in modern life "crisis"—a concept that "imposed
choices between stark alternatives" (2006: 358)—has become a "catch-
word" (358), reflecting a tendency for the pressure to make decisions
under conditions of uncertainty to become generalized and percolate
into the structure of everyday consciousness. Not making decisions is
not an option: there is no safe position that does not require making
investments and engaging contingency—life needs to defeat entropy to
stave off decline and postpone death. In this respect Luhmann always
remained at some distance from the claims of process philosophy and its
notion of duration; it correctly points out that temporality is immanent

and relative to the system, but it is not sufficiently attuned to the element of decision and the dynamics that produces, the way autopoiesis works through the constant disruption of immanence by self-reference, the paradoxical fact that the present attains a capacity for duration *even as* it becomes point-like. Self-organization works through the active engagement of contingency and the continuous transgression of existing limits.

Decision involves the subject's repositioning itself within the mechanisms that switch the past into the future, that is, the need to reassess our past and recalibrate our expectations and adjust our portfolio of speculative investments. The distinctive logic of temporalization that governs the dynamics of capitalism is best reflected in the rules of double-entry bookkeeping, an accounting technique that emerged in the secularizing context of the Italian Renaissance and that still provides one of the main devices through which the capitalist economy organizes knowledge of itself (Levy 2014: 174–75). Double-entry bookkeeping has often been associated with the rise of capitalism (Weber 1978; Carruthers and Espeland 1991), but such arguments have tended to emphasize the symbiotic relation between accounting rules and the rationalizing thrust of the market without explaining why this, rather than another form of accounting, emerged. I argue here that the logic of the balance sheet can be seen as expressing and formalizing a particular relation to time; it is a device that operationalizes the distinction between past and future and so makes available a way to represent and manipulate the temporal structure of claims and obligations.

The balance sheet records on the right-hand side an actor's sources of funds and on the left-hand side the uses to which she has put them. The principle that double-entry bookkeeping codifies in this way is that a subject can make promises (that is, incur debts) and invest the cash proceeds of those commitments (their present value, made available as credit) in promises made by others. The existence of a double-entry bookkeeping system only makes sense because the world does not resemble a neoclassical market that works through instantaneous adjustments. In

a neoclassical world, there is no point in thinking of balance sheets, because the balance between sources and uses of funds (between liabilities
and assets, between the obligations incurred in the past and how we have
invested them) can never be precarious. It is only in a world of uncertain
investments that funds get tied up in consequential ways; investments
need to generate sufficient revenue to permit the investor to keep up
with the payments on her debt. It is crucial to appreciate the constitutive
dimension of this process: if contractual commitments were regulated
by fundamental values, with time and expectations just practical issues
to be discounted objectively, then depicting the temporal transformation
of assets in this way would be a pointless, purely descriptive exercise—
bookkeeping in the pejorative sense, perhaps of academic interest—but
there would have been no reason for it to have been originated by Italian
merchants. Balance sheet accounting is motivated by a recognition that
the valuation of commitments and obligations is malleable.[1]

CHAPTER 7

Minsky beyond the Critique of Speculation

The logic of the balance sheet is a key point of reference in Minsky's theorization of capitalism. Minsky is of course best known as the quintessential critic of speculation, and in the aftermath of the financial crisis the term "Minsky moment" has been widely adopted to refer to the moment when an unstable, top-heavy structure of speculative fictions begins to collapse. Although this book makes no claims about the "correct" interpretation of Minsky's work, it does argue that his work also offers insights pointing in a quite different direction, ones we can exploit to move beyond the limitations of post-Keynesian theory. Minsky is acutely aware that *all* investments are to some degree speculative in the sense that their success or failure will only be determined in an unknown future: "the essence of capitalism is that units have to take positions in an uncertain world" (1980: 515). Similarly, "ignorance and conjecture enter decisions to create and finance capital assets whose value, once they are in place, depends upon the markets' view of their prospective returns over a long horizon" (1996: 359).[1] For Minsky, the problem of economy relates to how the interaction of speculative investments generates order, a stable financial measure.

Minsky understands economic units as balance sheet entities, clusters of promises received and promises made. The dynamics of capitalism

are generated by subjects taking positions on the future, by speculative
investments with uncertain outcomes (Mehrling 2015). In modern life
a "clean" (nonspecious) present, enjoying fully cleared markets and un-
encumbered by past commitments and future expectations, is an impossibility. Economic actors issue obligations and use the cash proceeds to
make investments (Minsky 2008 [1986]: 47). They need to generate sufficient revenue (cash flow) from their investments to be able to service
their debts in accordance with the agreed-upon repayment schedule. In
Minsky's understanding of balance sheet dynamics, the notion of liquidity therefore plays an important role (Nesvetailova 2014: 136); it refers to
the ability to meet obligations as they become due. If someone is about
to fall foul of the payment constraint and is unable to access a new source
of finance or roll over existing ones, he will be forced to sell off assets.
In other words, if one's liquidity is compromised, one may have to sell
assets even if they have a perfectly good chance of working out over the
longer run. The payment constraint is a veritable "survival constraint," a
term recovered by Mehrling (1999: 139) from Minsky's doctoral thesis.

The notion of solvency, by contrast, refers to the quality of a balance
sheet if assets were given indefinite time to work out. As such, it reflects
the way the idea of fundamental (timeless) value is operationalized in
the practice of financial balance sheet analysis. What Minsky's understanding of balance sheet dynamics allows us to see is that we cannot
meaningfully think about financial value separately from the temporal
logic of liquidity and payment. In Minsky's thinking, solvency ceases to
be an inflexible bottom line, but becomes something that is profoundly
shaped by decisions regarding the shifting of payment constraints. If
we enjoy an infinite deferral of repayment pressures, even the most ill-
advised investments will work out, just by the sheer logic of chance (it's
as if we were assured however much credit we need to pick the winning
lottery ticket). Here it is crucial to recognize that nothing is automatic
about the operation of the liquidity constraint: its enforcement always
involves a moment of judgment and decision. If a creditor perceives that
extending further credit is likely to lead to repayment in the end, it is in

her own interest to provide such funding. In that sense, for Minsky cash flow is "the most basic element and the ultimate reality of the system" (Mehrling 2000a: 82).[2]

The interactive logic of speculative investments and fictitious claims is characterized by a particular process of punctualization: it becomes oriented around and stabilized by a financial standard, a monetary measure. In depicting how balance sheet interactions generate money, Minsky assigns a crucial role to banks. Banks were, in origin, firms settling payments and clearing debts and credits, offering ways to economize on the use of money. Instead of noncommittal, fee-based brokerage services, this often involved taking the assets of other economic actors onto their own balance sheet. A bank is a "dealer in debts or credits" (Hawtrey 1922: 4; cf. Baecker 1991: 49). In this way, banks came to serve as nodal points in the payments network, and the promissory notes they issued would often begin to circulate without being presented for redemption, leading banks to capitalize on this by issuing more credit (notes or deposits) than they had cash on hand (so-called fractional reserve banking). A bank thereby makes a market for its own obligations (Mehrling 2000b: 366), and its notes serve as a measure, a promise against which the value of other promises is assessed. What occurs is an endogenous hierarchization of valuation practices. Capitalist money, then, is bank debt (Wray 1990; Ingham 2004). Financial order is not produced through arbitrary numerators, or symbolic devices instituted by fiat, but it emerges organically out of the interaction of credit relations and the payment pressures they produce. The bank and its promises create an element of stability in the logic of temporal transformations.

Banks are institutions that specialize in leveraging (Sgambati 2015); they buy up existing promises by issuing their own short-term commitments. They accept a large number of heterogeneous promises already made in commercial interactions and substitute for these their own promises to pay on demand.[3] A bank organizes specularity from within; it does not eradicate uncertainty but precisely leverages off uncertainty

by offering its commitments as a relatively safe asset in a contingent
world, as the least uncertain form of secular value. It does not in any
way rise above the logic of risk but bends that logic around itself. It
enjoys no special foresight but positions itself in such a way that its
promises come to function as a standard, allowing for the formation
of a calculative logic that can serve as an economic infrastructure. The
bank enjoys a kind of agency premised on its centrality as a reference
point for other agencies—that is, leverage. Economic actors become invested in the bank's infrastructure because participation in the temporal
logic it organizes offers the best chances for their own survival. Holding
the unit in which the value of other assets is denominated constitutes
a form of insurance: by holding money, we minimize our exposure to
unforeseen sources of risk. Money allows us to postpone decisions until
we have a better idea of what we need to do. It allows us to preserve
possibilities and options (Esposito 2011: 49–51; Shackle 1972: 206–7;
Davidson 2006: 141; Luhmann 1988: 268). "Money looks forward. It is
wanted so that it can be later exchanged for something whose precise
nature need not now be decided" (Shackle 1972: xv). It is a technology
for handling the secular condition of risk.

Like many other economic units, banks issue short-term obligations
to fund longer-term investments; but they are distinctive because in-
flows and outflows are denominated in the bank's own obligations. A
bank can borrow without having to find a particular lender; its lenders
are the community that accepts its promises as currency (Desan 2015).
This ability to create liquidity loosens the bank's payment constraint,
which at the same time confers on the bank a capacity for loosening the
survival constraints of other economic units. Banks occupy a privileged
position in the production and distribution of secular temporality. If
a regular (nonbank) economic unit is successful, its promissory notes
may gradually be recognized as less risky and more desirable than those
of others and trade at a premium, but this will merely mean a shift of
financing, that is a loosening of the cash constraint for that unit which
will be accompanied by a tightening of the cash constraint elsewhere.

Multiplier banking does not just redistribute exposure to an existing cash constraint but also alleviates that constraint at an aggregate level. Banks command a power to make available time.

From a neoclassical point of view, all this would seem to be putting the cart before the horse; by its reasoning, the possibility of balance sheet operations (that is, the creation of credit and debt) presupposes a monetary standard in which payments can be denominated. Minsky's point is precisely that we need to understand the emergence of that standard itself as a historical process. If there is a certain circularity at play here, it is not a nonsensical intellectual contradiction, but it reflects the fact that money is self-referential. On the one hand, money is produced endogenously: no external measure preexists the dynamics of economic interaction, and it needs to be reproduced continuously. On the other hand, money has a constitutive impact on the financing practices out of which it emerges and in this sense takes on an element of autonomy that can easily be mistaken for exogeneity. Money becomes autopoietic, capable of reproducing itself through its own operations.

But it is by no means *destined* to do so. Although in this book I have emphasized the role of leverage in the endogenous stabilization of contingency, and so positioned that concept to contrast with its established meaning in critical approaches as a source of instability, this is certainly not to deny that leveraging can have destabilizing effects. Prevailing interpretations of Minsky's (1977) "financial instability hypothesis" center on his characterization of financing structures, attributing instability to the move away from nonspeculative "hedge" financing (seen as grounded in the real value of material production) and the growing reliance on "speculative" and eventually "Ponzi" financing structures.[4] But to assess instability and its causes against the ideal image of a nonspeculative capitalism is, as this book has argued, a debilitating move. Not only does hedge financing too contain an inevitably speculative element, but such interpretations also sit uneasily with Minsky's understanding that the speculative financing structure of borrowing short and lending long is the distinctive business model of the banking system and how

it generates money.[5] A more fruitful take on the production of financial instability is formulated in what has been termed "post-Keynesian
institutionalism," which rejects the dichotomization of real economy
and finance. It recovers the influence of Commons's notion of futurity
on Keynes's work and reads Minsky's contributions through this lens
(Atkinson and Whalen 2011; Nesvetailova 2015). The dynamic identified here has to do with the way the self-referential character of specular
valuation engenders a mutually reinforcing connection between asset
appreciation and the ability to borrow and leverage: the appreciation of
assets through speculation permits the owner to access new credit that
can be used to finance new speculative investments, in turn driving up
the prices of those assets. This phenomenon has been referred to as the
"procyclical" nature of leverage, that is, the tendency of specular valuation to feed on itself (Palan 2013, 2015). The procyclical dynamics of
capitalist finance push outward, creating their own sources of contingency: growing complexity builds capacities for adaptation but simultaneously multiplies the number of connections that can fail.

That banking never eradicates uncertainty and that money never
becomes an absolute standard of value or external measure becomes apparent when confidence in a bank's promissory notes falters and a bank
experiences a sudden withdrawal of short-term financing (a "run on the
bank"), which quickly tightens its payment constraint. By virtue of its centrality in the payments network, the bank comes to function as an agent
of contagion. This typically works through a freezing of the interbank
market: the inability of one bank to meet its payment obligations will
quickly impair the ability of other banks to meet their obligations, leading
them to sell off assets against steep discounts, thereby putting downward
pressure on their value and triggering a deleveraging movement. In the
deleveraging of the financial game and the unwinding of credit positions,
it becomes clear how plastic our relation to the present and the past is
and how quickly we revalue practices and projects. The self-expansionary
logic of valuation that was organized around the bank turns into its oppo-
site, and credit becomes very hard to obtain—identities that only recently

seemed to have a secure future are now suddenly deemed to lack value and find themselves cut off from credit.

In precapitalist Europe, bank crises often resulted in a complete collapse of bank-centered financial networks, leading rulers to impose wholesale bans on multiplier banking (Kohn 1999). But with the development of capitalist finance in England, crises often served as paradoxical occasions for accelerated hierarchization, spurring a wider logic of financial organization (Knafo 2013). Even though the capitalist landscape looks like a complex constellation of overlapping standards and measures, this is characterized by a definite dynamic of hierarchization, with new forms of banking not just emerging alongside existing ones, but also layering themselves on top of those (Mehrling 2000b; Bell 2001). An important development in this process was the emergence of bankers' banks, such as the Bank of England, which related to regular banks in the same way as the latter related to the public (Hawtrey 1932: 116). Over time the Bank of England came to function as a "lender of last resort," alleviating the liquidity pressures and payment constraints that banks experienced during crises and thus allowing them to meet their obligations without having to sell off their assets and thereby becoming a source of contagion (Bagehot 1962 [1873]; Hawtrey 1932). When a bank became subject to a drain on its reserves, the Bank of England would temporarily take some of the bank's assets on its own books, so providing it with liquidity and time and allowing it to meet its obligations. That is, the lender-of-last-resort function seeks to prevent the procyclical logic of balance sheet contractions from working itself out: "the lender of last resort short-circuits the need of the institution in difficulty to acquire funds by selling out its position in financial and real assets, which can lead to sharp declines in asset values" (Minsky 2008 [1986]: 49). With each crisis the promissory notes of the Bank of England came to occupy a more central position in the system as a whole, and the transformation of these key private banks into public institutions was driven by the awareness of the possibilities for governance and system stabilization that the latter made available. The adoption of national currencies through the conferral on central banks of a monopoly on note issue further enhanced the ability of central banks to perform their lender-of-last-resort functions by further "powering" their obligations (Hawtrey 1932: 131).

For Minsky, there is no clear dividing line between practices of banking and their governance; no qualitative break exists between the ordinary logic of risk navigation and the management of system risk. Financial authority should be understood not as imposed externally but as arising organically out of the ordering principles internal to economic processes. Central banking does not represent a means of exogenous regulation but is itself a form of banking, and in many respects it follows a similar logic of operation. When a bank comes under pressure, the response is never an across-the-board credit contraction; large borrowers, too-big-to-fail constituents, are the last to experience the contraction of credit and can count on the most accommodation. Central banking similarly responds to the particular topological properties exhibited by financial networks, that is, the existence of financial nodal points and the possibility that their failure will take down wider social structures. The central bank's ability to safeguard the integrity of the system as a whole is centrally predicated on its capacity for risk shifting, the selective socialization of risk (Minsky 2008 [1996]: 49). A too-big-to-fail logic based on backstopping and bailout is thus a core feature of capitalist financial management, which is something that Minsky understood very well and led him to be highly skeptical toward claims of discretionary precision management made on behalf of modern monetary policy. As he put it, "Unless the economy is such that depression-inducing financial instability would occur from time to time in the absence of Federal Reserve intervention, the Federal Reserve System is largely superfluous" (Minsky 2008 [1986]: 49; cf. Hawtrey 1932). Or as Aglietta and Scialom put it, last-resort lending is "the gist of the art of central banking" (2008: 4).

But this awareness of the inherent limitations of central bank interventions (their inability to transcend the logic of banking and manipulate the financial system from without) never led Minsky to doubt the efficacy of the central bank, its ability to perform the functions that were organically embedded in its constitution. The endogenous nature of financial policy is something of a double-edged sword. On the one hand, it means that the governance of finance always falls short of an imagined version that works through external observation and intervention and delivers a neutral financial structure. Financial governance is forever plagued by its embeddedness, the impossibility of cleanly extricating itself from the processes it seeks to regulate. On the other hand, the fact that financial authority is not an external imposition but is organically connected to lower-level financial practices means that at times of intense uncertainty it can operate with considerable efficiency, relying on existing chains of connections. The central bank responds to strains in the financial operations that connect it to other banks as these make themselves apparent in the payments system. The process of financial management can accordingly appear remarkably banal: when risk spreads and becomes a systemic threat, there is little to be done other than fortify the key nodes of the payments system. Central banking is about the rearrangement and redistribution of the liquidity pressures generated by existing contractual commitments, making new contractual options available to a select number of financial institutions to allow them privileged access to refinancing and thus alleviate their survival constraint. This means that a constitutive asymmetry is at the heart of financial management: the central bank's protections redound not democratically but to those institutions that function as financial hubs and have gathered sufficient power that their survival is of systemic importance. In that sense, "too big to fail" is the core operational modality of central banks. It works to give some identities more time than others.

CHAPTER 8

Practices of (Central) Banking, Imaginaries of Neutrality

These Minskyan themes allow us to see clearly what is wrong with the neo-classical conception of money, which reduces the problem of temporality to the problem of coordination that emerges in an economy based on barter and then posits money as a one-off solution, a neutral device that can function as an external measure and remain beyond the specular logic of measure and valuation. The Minskyan critique of this idea revolves around the notion that money is produced through banking mechanisms that stabilize the logic of specularity from within, and so exerts specific organizing effects on the field of financial obligations. "Non-neutrality of money arises as a natural consequence of the fact that money is a debt of banks brought mainly into being as banks finance business" (Minsky 1986: 352). And yet historically it was precisely amid the rise of capitalist banking that the idea of money as a neutral device emerged and acquired intellectual and political traction. Of course, the idea of the neutrality of money is not entirely without premodern antecedents. Perhaps some version of it can be seen to go back as far as Aristotle, whose distinction between economy and chrematistics provided a guide to the appropriate and inappropriate uses of money. But what Aristotle emphatically did not say—and quite possibly could not have conceived of—was that money could ever be neutral, a technology that was essential to the self-organization of human society yet somehow did not exert any regulatory powers. To his mind, the danger of unnatural chrematistics was ever present, even in the appropriate use of money. Similarly, medieval theologians could never have said that money was in principle neutral, merely an innocuous convention: it was a pretentious fiction that *at best* remained relatively harmless. There was a slippery slope from interest to usury, and the former was never above suspicion.

It is only in modern capitalism that we find a conception of money as neutral, pure instrumentality, a clean way of attaining a goal, without effects of its own. There is a real paradox here. The orthodox conception of money as a simple numeraire is to some extent applicable to simple economic situations, where actors meet to exchange commodities for mutual benefit and are neither encumbered by commitments inherited from the past nor minded to leave with debts or credits—what Minsky referred to as the "village fair" model (1982: 61).[1] But it is especially in a capitalist context, where the logic of instantaneous exchange becomes dominated by the dynamics of temporally situated investments and credit and debt, that the orthodox conception of money becomes principally untenable. Yet it is precisely at this juncture that it arises. Much of the history of modern finance can be understood in terms of the tension between, on the one hand, the endogenous character of money (the fact that it is produced through banking and leveraging mechanisms that organize specularity from within) and, on the other hand, the fantasy that we can exogenously define what money is and unambiguously distinguish it from not-money, bypassing the logic of economic self-organization.

We can trace the doctrine of monetary neutrality back to the Scottish Enlightenment. Because of a chronic shortage of specie, finance in eighteenth-century Scotland was more highly developed than in England. Seeking to counter the perennial meddling of the British state in Scottish financial institutions, thinkers such as David Hume and later

Adam Smith sought to provide a justification for the widespread use of
paper money. Arguing that the creation of money tokens was perfectly
acceptable in cases where this could facilitate sound objectives of commercial interaction, they insisted that money was simply a convention
and that its availability should not be arbitrarily and needlessly constrained (Knafo 2013: 119). Money was a mere numeraire that made
things commensurable, a passive measure without constitutive effects
on what it measured—that is, "only the instrument which men have
agreed upon to facilitate the exchange of one commodity for another"
(Hume 1985 [1752]: 281). Of course, Hume and Smith still associated
money proper with a metallic standard, as would many thinkers after
them. But their reasons for doing so differed from those of the mer-
cantilists. Whereas the latter had fetishized gold and silver (and naïvely
thought that the mere accumulation of these metals could secure a nation's wealth), for Hume and Smith specie was simply a commodity that
had historically come to serve as a standard of value.

Hume was nonetheless ambivalent about banks: even as he acknowl-
edged that they had liberated Scotland from an artificial lack of gold
money, he mistrusted their tendency to issue paper money beyond those
requirements (Arnon 2011: 22). According to Hume's quantity theory,
the amount of paper money in circulation should be a one-to-one representation of the amount of specie required to lubricate the wheels
of commerce. In other words, Hume was tolerant of banks only insofar as they would not engage in fractional reserve banking. In this way,
his economic thought was characterized by a strong tension between a
belief in the conventionality of money and an opposition to the actual
banking practices that had made this conventionality apparent and had
brought its potential benefits onto the political and intellectual agenda.
Smith's theory of money and banking can be seen as addressing this
problem (Knafo 2013: 119): his real bills doctrine outlined a specific criterion for the legitimate extension of credit that would ensure the consistency of banks' lending practices with monetary neutrality. According
to the real bills doctrine, banks could safely extend credit on the basis of

bills secured by mercantile transactions (such bills were considered to be "self-liquidating" because the delivery of the goods would automatically furnish the means for the repayment of the bill). The doctrine was seen as ensuring that the amount of paper money circulating would be equal to the amount of metal currency that would have circulated in the absence of symbolic representations of money. By providing a specific criterion to separate legitimate from illegitimate engagement of the future, Smith made the idea of neutral money consistent with banking and the dealing in future-oriented obligations.[2]

Whereas in premodern times conceptions of money had been inextricably bound up with the critique of speculation, the new conception of monetary neutrality disarticulates these. Even if specific financial forms continue to attract charges of irrationality, money *as a concept* becomes exempt from that critique. Moderns still criticize specific kinds of investments and financial arrangements for their speculative character, but criticizing the very concept of money has become harder; the idea that we could hope to live without the commensurating and calculating functions of some kind of money comes to seem somewhat naïve or immature. Money is no longer seen as a corrupting force but instead as a principally innocuous symbol that can *itself* become corrupted by bad-faith speculative practices. Whereas in the past political and religious ordering principles needed to be safeguarded from the corrupting influence of money, in the modern conception it is precisely money itself that needs such protection. The critique of speculation now becomes crucial precisely as a means to safeguard the symbolic innocence of money; whereas in premodern times any attempt to deal in futurity was suspect, in modern life we subject speculative investments to much more fine-grained assessments, continuously making distinctions between legitimate and illegitimate fictions (Lears 2003).

The notion of monetary neutrality should thus be seen as the ideological expression of a secular economic rationality that recognizes the inevitability of speculative investments; together with the emerging legitimacy of secular time arises the idea that time can be neutralized and

that money can be neatly and exogenously defined. At work here is a
Kantian leap: a discovery of the productive nature of monetary representation that is immediately attended by a fantasy of the self-transparency
of such representation. Moderns readily realize that money serves as an
organizing moment in the interactive logic of contingent claims and
speculative positions, and in this sense it clearly does something and is
productive; but this very productivity is disavowed as money is held to
be nothing but a passive symbol, merely faithfully representing foundational values. This speaks to the ease with which the modern imaginary
is able to switch back and forth between on the one hand a recognition
that economic life is "constructed"—speculative and performative—and
on the other hand a conviction that financial forms and signs should
reflect foundations.

We should not be too quick to associate the imaginary of neutrality with procapitalist ideology or the particular beliefs of professional
economists. It has a strong republican valence, promising a market
structure that protects society from concentrations of power and the arbitrary exercise of authority.[3] Throughout modern financial history, we
see the reemergence of attempts to ensure the neutrality of money by
defining it in a way that bypasses the logic internal to the banking system. This was evident in the foundation of the Federal Reserve System,
when the real bills doctrine came to serve as a key argument to reassure
the American population that the signs it would issue would be neutral,
reflecting the productive foundations of the American economy rather
than advancing the self-serving speculative schemes of New York financial elites (West 1977). It is also evident in the considerable populist
credentials the quantity theory has always enjoyed (Laidler 2004a), and
in the fact that during the 1970s monetarist notions of quantity targets
for monetary growth were pushed onto the policy agenda by populist
interests in Congress (see also the discussion in the next chapter).

Smith considered the real bills doctrine an important argument
against the concentration of power in a central bank (Arnon 2011: 43–
44), which he viewed as a ready way for vested interests to protect their

own positions, leading only to an overissue of money that would feed inflation and undermine the soundness of the currency. But the rationality of risk is not easily contained within the parameters of a specific doctrine, and Thornton pointed to the practical limitations of the distinction between real and fictitious bills (Mints 1945: 52). He considered it unlikely that merchants and banks were always able to tell the difference between the two, nor was it necessarily in their own interest to avoid speculative bills, as Smith had mistakenly assumed (Arnon 2011: 101–2). For Thornton, even in mercantile transactions the role of credit was still predicated on confidence and expectations (1965 [1802]: 75). He thus challenged the notion that paper money should be thought of strictly in relation to the metallic currency that would have circulated in the absence of paper (95). There was no reason to think that bank-issued paper should simply be a one-to-one, linear representation of metallic coin: it played its own constructive role, facilitating productive events that otherwise might not have materialized.[4]

Thornton was well aware that the flipside of this productive non-neutrality of bank credit was the instability that it caused, and he placed great emphasis on the role of the central bank in the stabilization of the banking system. Whereas Smith had viewed central banking as corrupting the logic of the market, Thornton's more benevolent assessment was rooted in an appreciation of the hierarchizing dynamics of the credit system and the way these had organically evolved to position the Bank of England at their center. For Thornton, a sudden contraction in the volume of paper money was no less serious a problem than the overissue of paper money. If there was a problem with the way the Bank of England functioned, it was precisely that it did not do enough to counteract the deleveraging and deflationary effects of crises. During a crisis the central bank should expand its lending, and it was the pernicious influence of the real bills doctrine—which counseled a procyclical contraction of credit at a time of business slowdown, thus reducing the overall amount of means of payment available for commercial activity and reinforcing the downturn—that hobbled the Bank's ability to act decisively to stabilize the financial system. In this way, Thornton provided a conceptual basis for the notion of the lender of last resort, which had been advanced first by Sir Francis Baring (1967 [1797]) several years earlier.

Observers of central banking have always been aware to some extent of the "moral hazard" these kinds of policies entail—the fact that by supporting banks deemed to be systemically significant, central bank policies amplify leveraging dynamics and sustain the practices that gave rise to instability in the first place. Concerns, such as those voiced by Smith, that the kind of policy arrangements Thornton advocated would primarily redound to the benefit of vested financial interests never disappeared. This did much to shape the debates that would dominate much of English financial policymaking in the nineteenth century, which revolved around the question of how to ensure the neutrality of the currency in a context where it was increasingly widely accepted that the inner mechanisms of modern finance generated instability.[5] Bagehot's formulation of the lender-of-last-resort doctrine toward the end of the nineteenth century can be seen as a sort of compromise position in this respect. He defined the role of the lender of last resort in terms of the central bank's willingness to lend freely, but at an interest rate premium and only against well-secured financial assets. Those stipulations were meant to ensure that banks would only avail themselves of the central bank's lending facilities during a crisis, when no other sources of finance were available, and so to protect against their abuse.

But this was never an exhaustive response to the problem of moral hazard; it did little to prevent banks from taking more risk during good times, because they could expect to be bailed out if they got into trouble. Furthermore, the insistence on good collateral as a condition of last-resort lending provides little guidance when the problem consists of more than a superficial liquidity bottleneck and when the quality of the collateral is precisely in question. As Hawtrey put it, "The insolvency may be so widespread, that advances limited to good security may do little or nothing to save the situation" (1919: 153). In other words, the Bagehot doctrine was problematically premised on the possibility of clearly distinguishing liquidity problems from solvency problems (Goodhart 1999). A Minskyan appreciation that solvency and asset values have no existence independent of the dynamics of liquidity and payment suggests that financial governance can never be neutral: the selective provision of refinancing liquidity is a way of sustaining certain values rather than others. Last-resort lending, consequently and for good reason, has never been able to rise above moral and political suspicion.

The ability to influence processes of credit expansion and contraction to forestall the need for lender-of-last-resort assistance has therefore always been the holy grail of central banking. In this respect central bank practitioners have always been aware of the limitations of formal quantitative and qualitative principles, such as the Humean quantity principle or the Smithian real bills doctrine, which they consider insufficiently attuned to the endogenous dynamics of the banking system—such principles have often been more popular among those who seek to constrain the discretionary powers of central bankers. Of greater influence has been the idea of countercyclical policy as it was first formulated by Wicksell (1962 [1898]). Wicksell is typically seen as the scholar who brought questions of time back into economic thought after they had been expunged by the marginalist revolution. But even though this means Wicksell's work has had considerable influence on the development of heterodox economic theory (Goodspeed 2012), it essentially considers how to bring time back in while neutralizing it in order to bring the world more fully in line with the neoclassical model. Wicksell thought in terms of the credit and debts entailed by temporally situated investments and argued that money could be effectively neutral if the nominal money rate of interest were kept equal to the natural rate (a fictitious construct, the return on capital if there were no need for money): "if money is loaned at this same rate of interest, it serves as nothing more than a cloak to cover a procedure which, from the purely formal point of view, could have been carried on equally well without it" (Wicksell 1962 [1898]: 104).

This was not a matter of defining money in ways that are at odds with the logic of the banking system or of imposing artificial criteria to limit the speculative character of positions, but rather of making shrewd use of a channel through which the central bank was organically connected to the financial system—the interest rate. Wicksell thus proposed an exceedingly simple way of securing the neutrality of money in a world without any constraints on credit or speculation. In his thought, financial governance became a tidy affair, able to dispense with the blunt instrument of lender-of-last-resort bailouts and merely requiring someone to set the correct interest rate. During the early twentieth century, instability was still such a pronounced feature of financial life, and the role of the central bank was so centrally defined by its lender-of-last-resort dimension, that the idea of a financial policy based primarily on the countercyclical adjustment of interest rates did not have all that much practical relevance (Wicker 1966). The technocratic fantasy of financial governance that Wicksell's work articulated (in which the discretionary agency of the central bank takes itself as capable of neutralizing the instabilities that had given rise to its existence) would come into its own later—not, however, because it superseded or made redundant the lender-of-last-resort function, but rather because the latter became institutionalized in the routine operation of financial policy. Whereas a nineteenth-century observer might have had difficulty relating to the idea that a central bank could have functions other than last-resort lending, a late-twentieth-century observer could similarly have been forgiven for assuming that central banking is essentially only about inflation targeting.

CHAPTER 9

Lineages of US Financial Governance

Although the Bagehot doctrine never provided a convincing theoretical solution to the problems associated with the lender-of-last-resort function, it nonetheless still had considerable relevance to the nineteenth-century context in Britain, where the large volume of trade-related debts provided a certain degree of stability for the banking system (Toniolo 2010: 63; Bignon et al. 2012). But the Bagehot doctrine never had much applicability in the context of the American system, which has always been inflected with a much stronger speculative dimension (Konings 2011) and never pivoted on trade-related bills (Hawtrey 1922: 226). Dynamics of leveraging and deleveraging were consequently a great deal more volatile, which meant that the need for a central bank was felt more urgently among bankers. But popular resistance, driven by sentiments that were not unlike Smith's feelings about central banks, time and again prevented the emergence or creation of such an institution (Timberlake 1993).

By the early twentieth century, crises got progressively more severe and the effects of financial instability were felt increasingly widely. Under these circumstances the case for a central bank became more compelling, and the Federal Reserve System was created in 1913. But the highly speculative character of the American financial system meant that its central bank faced particular challenges. On the one hand, the moral hazard problems it created were particularly pronounced: the prospect of the availability of last-resort lending gave a boost to banks' willingness to take risky financial positions (Degen 1987). On the other hand, it turned out that in the deleveraging movement the lender-of-last-resort function was not in fact all that effective: when financial dynamics are no longer governed even by a plausible notion of underlying value, intense doubt about the value of key securities sets in motion a fire-sale of bank assets that has no prospect of bottoming out and so continues to feed on itself (Calomiris and Mason 2003). In such situations, the provision of liquidity is entirely insufficient, as the crisis quickly appears to be one of solvency rather than mere liquidity. Simply put, during a crisis banks would have no sound collateral to offer (Wheelock 2010: 103), and lending on the principle of the Bagehot doctrine (even a considerably attenuated version of it) would therefore fail to arrest the deleveraging movement. These instabilities culminated in the crash of 1929 and the Depression, and the general crisis of capitalism.

The New Deal sought to create governance institutions that would improve the management of financial instability and actively work to prevent financial crises, but at the same time it needed to ensure the capacity of the system to respond to the growing popular demand for access to credit. The credit and securitization programs of the New Deal expanded the availability of government-assisted liquidity and made access dependent on investment in various forms of household debt (Hyman 2011). The government-sponsored enterprises essentially functioned as permanently available sources of liquidity, allowing banks to pass on their liquidity risk to a publicly supported institution. In addition, from the 1930s to early 1950s the effects of this were greatly magnified by the Federal Reserve's support for the market in government debt (Gaines 1962). At the same time, policymakers became more attuned to the practical impossibility of separating liquidity and solvency, leading them to focus on the technical logistics of the interbank payment system and seek to smooth out liquidity bottlenecks wherever they threatened to arise. All this amounted to the proactive provision of large amounts of liquidity to the banking system. But the major innovation of the New Deal was the introduction of deposit insurance, which undercut the rationale behind bank runs and fire-sales and prevented debt-deflation, thus serving as an integral part of the central banking function (Minsky 1982: 144, 2008 [1986]: 52). Insofar as the New Deal represented a class compromise, deposit insurance can be seen as its emblematic expression: it offers state guarantees of the funds of ordinary people while also greatly relaxing the survival constraints of banks, allowing them to engage in new forms of speculative, future-oriented credit extension (such as consumer credit and long-term mortgages for ordinary people). In other words, the New Deal reforms created what has come to be known as a "financial safety net" for the banking system (Schwartz 1987; Jones and Kolatch 1999).

This configuration of financial institutions transformed the dynamics of leveraging and deleveraging in significant ways, and the early postwar period saw no major meltdowns (Minsky 2008 [1986]: 50). The Federal Reserve now began to think of itself as conducting countercyclical policies, "leaning against the winds of deflation or inflation, whichever way they are blowing," as Chairman William McChesney Martin put it (quoted in Bremner 2004: 5). But of these, inflation would be the far bigger threat, and the Federal Reserve's ability to use interest rate increases to limit credit creation would always remain highly limited. The fact that banks were now protected to a significant extent from the threat of bank runs removed a certain symmetry between the leveraging and deleveraging mechanisms. The result was a permanent inflationary pressure (Minsky 2008 [1986]: 17). As Minsky put it, "Instead of a financial crisis and a deep depression being separated by decades, threats of crisis and deep depression occur every few years; instead of a realized deep depression, we now have chronic inflation" (Minsky 2008 [1986]: 106).[1] This created a distinctive set of governance challenges, which were reinforced by the fact that a variety of contracts, chief among them collective industrial agreements, had become indexed to inflation expectations. Although the postwar Federal Reserve viewed managing inflation as one of its main tasks, it was essentially counteracting the pressure that the New Deal arrangements had built into the system at large (Burns 1979).

When from the late 1950s the Fed became more actively concerned about inflation and sought to place restrictions on banks' abilities to create credit, banks invented new financial forms and techniques that remained outside the regulatory remit of the central bank. In a pattern that would repeat itself numerous times over the next decades, the Federal Reserve would move to develop some degree of regulatory control over these new areas of credit creation, only to face another set of financial innovations (Mayer 1974). Minsky (1957) was one of the first commentators to perceive these changes and the challenge they posed to the central bank. He viewed them primarily as a rebuttal of the Fed's pretenses of precision management, a reminder that the basic operational logic of financial management consisted in the stabilization of the payment network and last-resort lending. The accuracy of this assessment was borne out by the course of financial management during the 1960s and 1970s: even as regulators were increasingly concerned about inflation, they saw no alternative to accommodating the financial practices that were responsible for the problem (Mayer 1999), expanding publicly sponsored options for securitization, increasing the level of protection for the payments system, and providing legal support for various forms of innovation—all of which fostered expectations of support among large financial institutions (Minsky 2008 [1986]: 221–22). Attempts to limit banks' creation of credit only served to fuel the growth of a shadow banking system, much of which could draw on these facilities. The result was a return to leveraging and deleveraging and increased instability. Extending insurance arrangements to the capital markets was not a viable option for both political and economic reasons, and so a future of ad hoc bailouts seemed to be in the offing. During the 1970s, as it became clear that even economic stagnation would not slow down inflation, the Federal Reserve increasingly understood the problem as sustained at basic operational levels of financial management.

Minsky seemed to feel there was no real way out of this predicament: short of a major political change that would democratize investment and the allocation of credit, there seemed to be no way for the American state to escape the kind of awkward dynamic it was constitutively embroiled in. These feelings were to some extent shared by Arthur Burns, Federal Reserve chairman for most of the decade. In a 1979 speech entitled "The Anguish of Central Banking," he complained that the Federal Reserve could not conquer inflation without generating a range of intolerable side-effects (1979: 16). Emphasizing that the Federal Reserve did not find itself in a position that permitted it to access clean policy solutions, he noted that during the previous decade "monetary policy came to be governed by the principle of undernourishing the inflationary process while still accommodating a good part of the pressures in the marketplace" (16). According to Burns, the problem had become highly psychological, bound up with expectations: "If the United States and other industrial countries are to make real headway in the fight against inflation it will first be necessary to rout inflationary psychology" (24). And he went on to argue that "Such a change in national psychology is not likely to be accomplished by marginal adjustments of public policy. In view of the strong and widespread expectations of inflation that prevail at present, I have therefore reluctantly come to believe that fairly drastic therapy will be needed to turn inflationary psychology around" (24).

Such therapy came soon after Burns left, in the guise of the turn to monetarism initiated by Paul Volcker. Monetarist doctrine can be viewed as a modern incarnation of Hume's quantity theory. To ensure that money functions in its neutral capacity, it proposes that the central bank maintain strict institutional control over the quantity of its creation (Friedman 1956). Many who led the adoption of monetarism as a Federal Reserve policy, chief among them Volcker himself, were skeptical about its merits as an economic theory (Silber 2012). But over the years, Congress had put considerable pressure on the Federal Reserve to take the idea of quantity targeting more seriously (Weintraub 1978). It is important here to appreciate the populist-republican credentials of monetarism, which were evident in the way its rise to prominence was aided by the campaigns of Congressman Wright Patman, who led popular sentiments that harbored a classic dislike of central banking and so became one of the main thorns in the side of the Fed (Kane 1975; Young 2000). The Federal Reserve's lack of accountability was for him a particular source of concern, and in this respect his concerns closely resembled those of monetarist thinkers (Weintraub 1977: 519). In his role as chairman of the Banking House Committee from 1963 he provided monetarist thinkers with a platform, and the hearings and reports he organized led to the passage in 1975 of a House resolution that encouraged the Fed to organize its monetary policy by measurable objectives, in particular the growth of monetary aggregates—a resolution that Milton Friedman viewed as central to the growing legitimacy of monetarism (Weintraub 1977: 526–27).

Forced to engage with the idea of quantity targeting, Volcker (1978, 1979) intuited its productive potential and practical uses. He was well aware that the state's lending and insurance functions were integral to the endogenous process whereby the dollar was constituted as a stable measure and were for that reason indispensable infrastructure; and he therefore did not consider replacing financial governance with a part-time operator guarding the quantity of money—as Friedman's (1982: 117) version of monetarism suggested—as a viable option. But at the same time, he saw the role of the state as a problem insofar as it contributed to inflation. In other words, Volcker perceived the problem as how the state might change the way it related to a process it was constitutively implicated in and could not just extricate itself from. This was not entirely different from how Minsky viewed things, but Volcker *did* see a way out that would not involve a wholesale democratization of investment. He looked to monetarism not as a means to enforce an external limit on the financial system, but as a means to affect expectations (cf. Kaplan 2003; Holmes 2013). He took it as a rhetorical device, as a way for the state to productively engage—rather than just accommodate— the endogenous dynamics of banking and money production.

This expectational aspect of monetarism was engaged in what Tobin (1980) termed "monetarism mark II," which referred to the way "new classical" economists reformulated its main arguments in a more qualitative register (Lucas 1972; Sargent 1982). On this reading, attempts to use inflationary monetary policy to advance social and political objectives tended to be incorporated into expectations, which meant that expansionary policies would merely result in inflation without generating their hoped-for beneficial consequences. Lucas (1976) separately formalized the argument regarding the futility of social engineering through discretionary financial policies, emphasizing the performative effects of policymaking: once an observed empirical regularity informs policy, that regularity will undergo change, so undermining the projected benefits of the policy. If Lucas's arguments appeared to reject any and all activist policies, the politics implicit in his argument were brought out clearly in Sargent's (1982) claim (supported by historical data showing that runaway inflation had only ever been conquered through some variety of shock therapy) that the turn to anti-inflationary policies needed to be preceded by a massive jolt of discipline. Although this line of thought is associated with new classical economics, it may make more sense, as Laidler suggests, to view Lucas and other defenders of neutral money through the prism of expectations as "neo-Austrians" (1981: 12).

CHAPTER 10

Hayek and Neoliberal Reason

If Volcker perceived the problem as how the state might change the way it related to a process in which it was constitutively implicated, we might say that he framed the problem of financial management along Hayekian lines: how is ordering possible if there is no political agency that can place itself outside of the logic of risk and speculation? Hayek's work contains a systems-theoretical or radical-constructivist problematic, which addresses how steering is possible in the context of an endogenously driven logic that rules out arbitrary, sovereign decisions and exogenous interventions (Cooper 2011; Kessler 2013). Although he referred explicitly to systems theory only later and occasionally (e.g., Hayek 1967: 22–42, 1979: 158), his work became substantively organized around the problematic of economic self-organization from the time he formulated his critique of socialist planning as a critique of rational constructivism (1937). In this way, Hayek's thinking foregrounded a problematic that led a more subterranean life in other strands of neoliberalism—how the awareness of the limits of rational constructivism could be internalized into practices of ordering and governing. The problem of economy as Hayek saw it bore close resemblance to the way Minsky framed it: the notion that "[u]ncertainty (or unsureness) is a deep property of decentralized systems in which a myriad of independent agents make decisions whose impacts are aggregated into outcomes that emerge over a range of tomorrows" is Minsky's (1996: 360) but could easily have been penned by Hayek. Yet their perspectives on the significance of this problematic diverged sharply. Whereas Minsky thought that only the socialization and coordination of investment decisions could provide a way out of the troublesome dynamics of the 1970s, to Hayek's mind it was precisely such ambitions for centralized control and rational economic engineering that were at the root of the problems capitalist society was facing in the first place.

At the core of Hayek's work is the notion that economic order can only arise through an evolutionary process of spontaneous self-organization: it cannot be rationally designed by an outside authority but must be an unintended effect of the competitive interaction of local entrepreneurial performances. We might understand Hayek's perspective on economic order as a more fully secularized version of Adam Smith's notion of the invisible hand. Although Hayek was deeply indebted to that idea, he nonetheless felt that Smith's conception had remained "metaphorical and incomplete" (1988: 148). If the metaphor of the invisible hand reflected an important intuition of the principles of self-organization and spontaneous ordering, to Hayek's more fully secularized mind it still smacked too much of a belief in divine trickery. Hayek categorically denied the possibility of outside interventions or steering and viewed economy as driven by nothing but trial and error, uncertainty and discovery. Whereas Smith advanced his famous metaphor to think about how order might still be possible in a secularizing world that can no longer see itself as governed by a divine mind, Hayek proposed his understanding of spontaneous order not to address a concern about the limitations of secular reason but precisely to respond to its "conceit" (1988), namely the faith in rational constructivism that he saw as the defining characteristic of twentieth-century socialism and progressivism. His claim was not just that acting without certainty or clear vision was acceptable but that it was necessary and imperative, that there is no source of order other than the engagement of risk and the interaction of speculative positions.

Summarizing the conclusion to which his turn to the problem of knowledge half a century earlier had eventually led him, Hayek in *The Fatal Conceit* insisted that only reason that "recognises its own limitations" and "faces the implications of the astonishing fact, revealed by economics and biology, that order generated without design can far outstrip plans men consciously contrive" is "reason properly used" (1988: 8). If Hayek viewed the problematic of economy in terms quite similar to Minsky's, and like him did not discern any possibilities for clean external interventions into its logic, he saw an intensified awareness of this very fact as itself the solution. The awareness of the impossibility of truly objective observations and real external interventions was *itself* the intervention that was needed. If for Hayek economy was a process of evolutionary emergence, he insisted that the resulting actants austerely recognize their secular origins and performative nature and refuse to abuse their reflexive capacities to entertain irrational fantasies of rational institutional design. Speculation was permitted and indeed required, but the subject should abandon any hope of transcending its partial and contingent nature and fully commit to the invisible logic of economy.

What prevented the modalities of economic self-organization from working well, according to Hayek, was precisely the way progressive ambitions for rational constructivism and social engineering interfered with them. What heterodox critics of contemporary capitalism often fail to discern is that neoliberal discourses *already* offer their *own* critique of exceptionalism, casting the progressive political project as an incoherent attempt to exempt the state from the risk rationality of the market. This critique sees the interventionist state (consisting on the one hand of the patronizing, progressive character who believes in rational design, and on the other hand of its beneficiaries, the people who cannot commit themselves to repaying their debts) as an improper, externally imposed obstacle to risk's ability to generate neutral, nonspeculative economic

foundations and unindebted money. Such reasoning attributes any economic problems to the fact that the market is "still" distorted by an external political agency that refuses to submit itself to the austere logic of
competitive evolution. This argument only gathers force every time it is
disproved, as such apparent evidence to the contrary only goes to show
that corruption runs even deeper than was previously realized. As Vatter (2014) argues, Hayek's philosophy has a strong republican valence:
deeply indebted to the thought of the Scottish Enlightenment (Horwitz
2001; Petsoulas 2001), his work was written at a time before it became
customary to distinguish republicanism from liberalism, imagining the
market above all as a source of protection against cumulative inequali-
ties or structural power differentials. Neoliberalism has always managed
to cast itself as the true heir to this republican vision of economy, allowing it to fold republican antigovernment sentiments into a governmental project.

The approach taken here to Hayek's politics thus differs from a
more familiar line of critique—one that views Hayek's work, and the
neoliberal project it articulates, as itself closely bound up with a sovereign decisionism in the tradition of Carl Schmitt, excepting itself
from the catallactic market dynamics that others presumably could not
escape (Cristi 1984; Scheuerman 1997; Papaioannou 2012; Bonefeld
2012). This reflects the more general tendency to ground the critique
of neoliberalism in an Agambenesque concern with its exceptional or
even authoritarian nature, and to argue that neoliberalism only sur-
vives through economic elites capturing the state in ways that enable
them to bypass democratic mechanisms of legitimation. To view Hayek
as embodying neoliberalism's hypocritical reliance on sovereign decisionism is to miss something important about a logic that is at work
both in his work and in neoliberal practice. Hayek, after all, is em-
phatic that the state has no privileged foresight and does not occupy
an exceptional space vis-à-vis the historical logic of economy.[1] The
Hayekian project is not to rehabilitate a sovereignty beyond risk but

to reactivate the self-organizing mechanisms that convert contingency into order—insisting on the preemptive generation, if need be, of the uncertainty that it takes to be the precondition of order (Davies and McGoey 2012). On this reading, neoliberalism involves not a resurgence of sovereign decisionism, but a recalibration of the connection between speculation and austerity as the axis of capitalist value. Whereas the idea of Schmittian exception is premised on the possibility of suspending the normalizing properties of risk and speculation, neoliberalism precisely relies on their operation. Aware that there is no outside to the logic of risk, it pushes at its boundaries in the expectation that such speculative transgressions will become integrated into the system's dynamics. It seeks to activate the normalizing properties of capitalist life by engaging the outer reaches of probability.

Here it is worth pointing out that Hayek never seemed to have a particular fascination with the figure of the entrepreneur. Whereas in Schumpeter's work entrepreneurs appear as the protagonists of capitalist development, Hayek seemed to view them simply as people doing their jobs without excuses or pretenses, participating in processes of information discovery by acting into an unknown future and so permitting the coordination of economic activities. No particular praise or attention seemed in order for this. Most of the time he seemed interested in another character, namely the person in debt to the past who had difficulty accepting this fact and was looking for excuses to get out of his repayment obligations. Hayek often seemed concerned to remind the subject of the obligations it inherited from the past, the servicing of which required an austere submission to forces beyond one's understanding. Here catallaxy did not appear as all that creative a process and involved little more than the matching of skills to tasks. Much of Hayek's work reads like an elaborate demolition of all the excuses the social-democratic subject has for questioning its predicament, like a rhetorically sophisticated belittling of the immature character that could not abandon its fantasies of the reconstruction of economic structures and sought to gain critical knowledge—the kind of nonvocational knowledge that is not directly serviceable to the operation of the economy. What Hayek offers is a critique of the critical impulse, a philosophical valorization of a sentiment— "Shut up and do your job"—that has always been at the heart of the ethos of neoliberalism.

In this way, Hayek's thought represents a paradoxical combination of future-orientation and reaction, manifesting the paradoxes of preemptive temporality. Even as he insisted that he was not a conservative because he was not opposed to change (see the postscript in Hayek [1960]), large parts of his oeuvre are devoted to the importance of tradition and customs, rules and pressures handed down from the past. The problems that modern capitalism was experiencing stemmed from the fact that people, under the influence of progressive and socialist political ideas, were increasingly reluctant to submit themselves to rules and institutions they did not understand. Incapable of appreciating the limits of social engineering, they childishly imagined that institutions should work according to reasons and intentions and that they should be able to know what kind of future they were making.[2]

It is worth taking a closer look here at the position that questions of money, banking, and finance occupy in Hayek's oeuvre. Hayek's (1933) early work, which developed ideas advanced earlier by Mises and Wicksell, dealt with issues of capital theory and business cycles, and it viewed instability as at its core a monetary phenomenon. It was characterized by an appreciation of the role of banks in the production of money and the logics of leveraging and deleveraging that it entailed. But this understanding of the nonneutrality of money creation and banking dynamics was still superimposed on and assessed against an orthodox notion of how money should work. Hayek grew weary of the attempt to square this circle, and during the war abandoned these issues to turn his attention to "more pressing problems" (Hayek quoted in Caldwell 2004: 180), above all the growing legitimacy of socialism and social democracy. Through his interventions into the socialist calculation debate, he developed a much more pronounced critique of neoclassical economics, a distinctive approach to economy as at its core a problem of knowledge (1949). Hayek recognized that on a neoclassical understanding of the problem of economy as a set of simultaneous equations, there was nothing inherently problematic about models of central planning, such as those formulated by Lange (1970 [1939]). Whereas Mises's contribution (1935) had still left some room for ambiguity, Hayek insisted that the problem with central planning went beyond practicalities (for instance, the absence of more powerful computers); rather, it was principally impossible for a central authority to know a future that was being made in real time.

Hayek did not seem to have much interest in using this theoretical framework to return to questions of money and instability. Had he done so, he might well have ended up with something very much like Minsky's theory, emphasizing the dynamic of instability, hierarchization, risk shifting, and the endogenous role the state plays in the financial system. But instead, Hayek abandoned economic theory for political philosophy and legal theory, and his work took a constitutionalist turn, seeing the proper role of social and political institutions as limited to providing abstract rules and theorizing law, in republican fashion, in terms of its ability to provide protections against state overreach. Singularly consumed with the threats to liberalism, he was concerned much more with the institutional preconditions of the market than with the temporal and topological properties of self-organizing processes themselves. Even as he contrasted the nonlinearity of catallactic self-organization with the orthodox idea of static equilibrium, he entirely lost interest in the question of financial instability, simply viewing it as the price of progress.[3]

It was amid the financial tumult and growing inflation of the 1970s that Hayek (1976a) finally returned to the financial question in a more specific way, arguing that the progressive state's transgression of its constitutional limitations had corrupted the market and its money. As a way out of financial instability, he counseled a full denationalization of money; anyone should be able to start up a bank and issue their own forms of money, the market deciding on the most appropriate currencies. Perhaps we can see Hayek here as continuing a line of thought that he cursorily outlined in his introduction to the 1939 reissue of Thornton's *Paper Credit*, where he remarked that Wicksell's work offered a more mature and complete treatment of the problematic Thornton had formulated (Hayek 1965 [1939]: 50). That may have been the main rationale for abandoning questions of money and finance for most of his career, but it was of course never a particularly satisfying solution. The idea that we can know the proper price of capital in advance of going through the information-generating mechanisms of the market process was entirely at odds with Hayek's own understanding of the role of knowledge in economic life. His proposal for a free-banking system seemed to be his way out of the problem, a way to let the market generate the knowledge that would stabilize it. Hayek readily admitted that a rhetorical sleight of hand was at work here—he initially raised the idea of free banking as a "bitter joke" (1979: 1)—but, he reported, the more he thought about it, the more satisfying he found the idea.

If Hayek now positioned banking as a kind of self-neutralizing activity and advocated engaging the future by returning to an imagined republican past of self-stabilizing free banking, this was blind to the practical difficulties that had beset free-banking experiments in history, notably the free-banking era in the United States. Here the work that Hayek had never done made itself felt, as this blocked a recognition that the role of the modern state in the production and definition of money *was* in fact the outcome of an evolutionary process characterized by its own internal rationality—a point that Minsky understood all too well. It was as if Minsky and Hayek were looking at the exact same phenomenon—the unregulated expansion of banking dynamics and the difficulty the Federal Reserve had in establishing some control over them—yet whereas the former saw nothing but problems and challenges, the latter also saw a highly promising proliferation of risk, a movement that was both disruptive and potentially restorative, simultaneously transgressive and normative. Whereas Friedmanian monetarism was fully invested in the possibility of formally defining a neutral money, Hayek was keenly aware that any attempt to constrain speculative logics was likely to be quickly undone by the expansionary logic of risk. Shadow banking could not be stably brought into the system overseen by a central bank; it could only be liberated. Such a liberation of banking dynamics was the point of the turn to monetarism.

CHAPTER 11

Neoliberal Financial Governance

Volcker saw the American financial system heading for a crisis of major proportions, one that would put it at the mercy of foreign investors who seemed to have growing doubts about the wisdom of holding US dollars. And he acted on this awareness by triggering a potentially productive crisis. The turn to monetarism was meant to provoke, driven by the intuition that a sudden policy turn could activate some of the financial system's endogenously situated ordering mechanisms. Volcker's move was offensively speculative—motivated not by a clear perception of the outcome of his moves but by an intuition of their productive, ordering potential. Far from the Federal Reserve making external interventions, it aggressively engaged the banking mechanisms of money production, creating new sources of uncertainty with a view to stabilizing the financial standard. Volcker was, to borrow Adkins's phrase again, "prospecting for potential" (2012: 625). In Volcker's hands, financial policy no longer simply served to align the state's operations with the logic of banking, whether in the reactive mode that had characterized financial policymaking until the early twentieth century or in the more preventative mode that characterized the post–New Deal era. Instead, it brought speculation into the operation of government. Neoliberalism signifies the movement of governmental rationality from a logic of anticipation and prevention to one of speculative preemption: it goes beyond a generic concern with the future and is oriented to the pragmatic uses of instability, uncertainty, and crisis, an embrace of the "ethic of the necessary decision in a context of uncertainty" (Ewald 2002: 294).

The Volcker program was a frantic and short-lived effort to measure and control the most relevant monetary aggregates through continuous interventions that needed adjusting as soon as they were implemented (Greider 1987). What was perfectly clear and predictable was that the policy turn would give rise to a dramatic expansion of the shadow banking system—which was why in the past the Fed had held back from such policies or quickly reversed them. The Volcker speculation consisted precisely in the wager that the instability caused by the Fed's persistence with those policies would set in motion wider political, economic, and social adjustments. The Volcker shock did not enforce an external limit on the creation of credit but activated some of the system's self-organizing mechanisms. The extent to which the success of Volcker's policies was bound up with a wider reconfiguration of the American political economy was illustrated by his (2000) confession that the Reagan administration's attack on organized labor had been crucial to the conquest of inflation (cf. Axilrod 2011: 99). And that was of course only one element in a wide-ranging set of policies that facilitated the accelerating destruction of the secure employment contracts of the Fordist manufacturing economy, and the dismantling of the limited public income provisions the New Deal had put in place. The resulting precarity of employment and remunerative austerity for the bulk of the American population offered a panoply of speculative opportunities, and the expansion of credit during recent decades has been deeply bound up with the growing difficulty of living off wages alone (Martin 2002; Lazzaratto 2009; Barba and Pivetti 2009; McCloud and Dwyer 2011). The neoliberal era has seen a dramatic growth of personal and household debt, much of it extended in ways and for purposes that earlier generations would have considered absurdly speculative. If twentieth-century

American capitalism had seen a progressive expansion of what speculative investments could be considered legitimate and of what could be constituted as a financial asset, the neoliberal era has greatly accelerated this process. In the aftermath of the turn to monetarism, the dollar emerged as a stable unit of value around which revolved an economy of accelerating speculation on proliferating contingencies—that is, as a more fully plastic, autopoietic sign.

Whereas the financialization trends of the Fordist era were still premised on the availability of steady paychecks and lifetime employment prospects, neoliberal financialization thrives precisely on the contingency of labor, its growing precarity (Ascher 2016). The tendency to think of neoliberalism as involving a recommodification of labor (as opposed to its partial decommodification effected during the era of Fordism) is problematic insofar as one of the key results of neoliberal restructuring is precisely the decrease in opportunities for straightforwardly exchanging one's labor for a wage (Adkins 2012; Cooper 2015). The neoliberal subject comes to think of his capacities, identity, and affinities as capital that requires valorization. He becomes a fully speculative unit, an "entrepreneur of himself" (Foucault 2008 [1979]: 226), under pressure to make the right decisions about the deployment of his credit under conditions of uncertainty. Foucault (2008 [1979]: 219–33) considered the notion of human capital (e.g., Becker 1964) as one of neoliberalism's main innovations; he viewed it as containing an implicit critique of the reification of labor, of the way classical political economy had reduced labor to a mere factor of production and neoclassical economics had subsequently reduced it to a generic technical parameter. In this respect, he seemed to suggest, the project of human capital theory has some unexpected parallels with Marx's critique of classical political economy and its concern to understand labor as a generative principle (Foucault 2008 [1979]: 220–21). The notion of human capital brings into view a broader, post-Fordist understanding of economic value and growth, one that is increasingly tied to interventions into the affective structure of subjectivity (232).

Feher (2009) has brought some important additional precision to Foucault's analysis by pointing out that neoliberal notions of human capital do not just relate to returns on investment but revolve more centrally around the possibility of capital gains, the appreciation of the investment. Above all, the neoliberal subject must ensure that its assets are speculated upon; its objective is "self-appreciation." This means that the imbrication of governance and subjectivity—the biopolitical dimension of neoliberalism's governmental rationality—becomes even more profound than Foucault recognized (cf. Lazzarato 2009, 2012): the neoliberal subject's aim is to make investments that induce investments, thereby positioning itself as a transmission point in a neoliberal rationality of simultaneous governmentalization and value generation. The subject develops a relation to itself that is speculative in the specific sense that this book has developed—it needs leverage, not just profits. But if the neoliberal subject faces the imperative of establishing itself as a bank of sorts, as a focal point in the interactive logic of speculative valuations that can benefit maximally from the procyclical logic of balance sheet expansion, it enjoys little protection from the downside of this process: few of us are too big to fail and we can count on relatively little accommodation when we run into difficulty maintaining payments on our debts.

The possibility of "transforming [one's] own risks into the dangers of all others" (Vogl 2014: 153) is the prerogative of large financial institutions. Even as neoliberal restructuring brought down inflation and alleviated pressure on the dollar, this was accompanied by significant financial volatility and a full-blown return to dynamics of leveraging and deleveraging. The 1980s saw a series of bailouts of systemically important institutions, and the expectations fostered in this way entailed the emergence of a too-big-to-fail regime (Hetzel 1991; Sprague 2000; Stern and Feldman 2004; Conti-Brown 2016: 154). Sufficiently large and critical financial institutions could do business in the expectation that if their speculations went sour the state would step in to alleviate their payments constraints. This amounted to an informal insurance regime for the shadow banking system, one that operated much more selectively than deposit insurance and so could avoid fanning inflation. Volcker may not of course have imagined the specific institutional contours of the too-big-to-fail regime as this emerged, but the very point of the neoliberal turn in financial management was to create a context where a more selective application of insurance principles—implying a more regressive form of risk socialization—would be politically and economically viable (Panitch and Gindin 2012: 179).

This new context entailed a shift in policymakers' attitude toward the issue of bailouts: the additional moral hazard that such repeated interventions would produce had been a major source of concern, but this gradually gave way to a pragmatic acceptance that periodic crises would continue to occur and that after-the-fact bailouts would have to play a role in containing their fallout (Athavale 2000). As Golub, Kaya, and Reay put it, during the neoliberal era the Federal Reserve increasingly focused on "post-hoc interventionism" (2015: 657), aiming to improve its ability to contain the effects of a crisis after it occurs. Panitch and Gindin (2012: 266) capture this development as a shift of concern from "failure prevention" to "failure containment," terms drawn from a 1998 report to Congress. Among Federal Reserve insiders this became known as the "mop up after" strategy (Blinder and Reis 2005: 70). If it was certainly recognized that this exacerbated moral hazard issues (that bailout interventions sustain and reinforce the very practices that brought on the need for them), this reflected not a moment of governmental irrationality but the fact that neoliberalism's preemptive rationality undermines any hard-and-fast distinction between problems and solutions.

This reorientation of the concerns of financial policymakers also had significant implications for the way policy was conducted during normal times. The Federal Reserve abandoned reservations about proactively using interest rate changes to alleviate liquidity pressures on large financial institutions (the "Greenspan put"), preventing market downturns through policies that sustained the practices responsible for instability (Ferguson and Jonson 2010). The growth of government-sponsored enterprises and the elaborate infrastructure of securitization techniques they supported did the same in a more unseen way, amounting to a significant expansion of permanently available public lending facilities that allowed financial institutions to liquidate their assets on an ongoing basis (Ashton 2011: 1803–4; Kolb 2011). Furthermore, the Federal Reserve, increasingly cognizant of the difficulty of treating questions of liquidity as separate from issues of solvency, became more engaged with the dynamics of the payment system and more alert to the need to proactively ensure its smooth operation. Now fully attuned to the importance of preventing the nervous system of American capitalism from freezing (Melzer 1986, 1995; Fullwiler 2003), the Federal Reserve identified a number of operational meanings of liquidity (such as payment system liquidity, settlement liquidity, funding liquidity, and rollover liquidity), allowing it to target a range of potential bottlenecks that could create system-level risks (Cecchetti and Disyatat 2010). Meanwhile, for all practical purposes policymakers were concerned not so much with reducing moral hazard but with enhancing resources for too-big-to-fail interventions and institutionalizing capacities for dealing with failing financial firms. In other words, the "federal financial safety net" underwent significant expansion during the neoliberal era (Malysheva and Walter 2010).

It is against this background that we should view what became known as the golden age of inflation targeting. The way neoliberal governance inhabits and deploys the tension between the necessity of speculation and the anticipation of a state of security was iconically expressed in the figure of Federal Reserve chairman Alan Greenspan, who oversaw the institutionalization of a regime of too-big-to-fail expectations but by all accounts seemed to genuinely believe that his policies were bringing America closer to a world of neutral money. This fantasy found considerable support in the remarkable performative properties his public utterances acquired, an apparent ability to initiate equilibrating market movements through announcements, safeguarding a noninflationary standard and a neutral marketplace through the performative magic of open-mouth operations. Monetary management at times appeared to have become an almost entirely rhetorical affair, in which the Fed could manage inflation through mere announcements of interest rate targets (Kaplan 2003; Holmes 2013). This self-image of neoliberal financial governance was formalized in the "new Keynesian" literature (e.g., Bernanke and Gertler 1999, 2001; Woodford 2003), which built on the new classical reorientation of economic theory to depict financial management as the control of inflation through the manipulation of expectations according to the Taylor rule (Kirshner 1999: 611; De Long 2000; Asso et al. 2007). The conception of central banking in its lender-of-last-resort function had no place in this frame of mind. As Laidler notes, although Woodford's *Interest and Prices* "to a greater or lesser extent informs the conduct of virtually all modern central banks, . . . the phrase 'lender of last resort' does not even appear in its index" (2004b: 4).

The practice and theory of neoliberal financial policy thus claimed to have fully realized the Wicksellian model, having found a way to produce a neutral monetary standard out of speculative, expectation-driven processes. This entailed not necessarily a naïve claim that bubbles—misvaluations that are not instantly corrected—could never occur, but rather an insistence that regulators were in no position to second-guess the market on this issue. The existence of a bubble could only be inferred after the fact, from the corrections emanating from the market itself. Whatever limited volatility still existed in the "age of moderation," many argued, could be dealt with by "mopping up after" (Blinder and Reis 2005; Posen 2006). For the rest, financial authorities should limit themselves to controlling inflation, paying attention to asset prices only insofar as they could cause inflation by increasing spending via the "wealth effect." But the notion that financial authorities had no business interfering with wider dynamics—that "[c]hanges in asset prices should affect monetary policy *only* to the extent that they affect the central bank's forecast of inflation" (Bernanke and Gertler 2001: 253)—always appeared more anxiously insistent than calmly confident: using policy instruments to sustain asset prices and to alleviate the liquidity constraints on highly leveraged financial institutions was precisely what the Greenspan Federal Reserve did on an ongoing basis. What found no expression in the new Keynesian depiction of financial management was the extent to which monetary policy had become bound up with such regressive risk shifting. Beneath the apparent magic of Greenspan's open-mouth operations could be found an elaborate operational infrastructure that effected an ongoing redistribution of payment constraints in favor of large financial institutions (cf. Issing 2009; Kane 2013).

The new Keynesian inflation-targeting framework never lacked for critics, who argued that it was possible to identify bubbles at least to some extent and argued for including some asset prices in the price indexes used to measure inflation (e.g., Goodhart 2001; Bell and Quiggin 2006; Roubini 2006). This was hardly unreasonable: the notion that a noninflationary currency could be achieved by institutionalizing asset inflation and bailouts through a semiseparate shadow banking system would no doubt have seemed absurd to someone like Wicksell. But such proposals went entirely against the neoliberal grain (see, for instance, Mishkin's [2006] strenuous objections, on the eve of the subprime crisis, against any deviation from the inflation-targeting framework established during the previous decades). Indeed, the removal of one key asset (home values) from the inflation index can be considered one of neoliberalism's more significant behind-the-scenes victories; it had originally been proposed in 1961 by the Stigler Commission (formally the Price Statistics Review Committee), but it was not until the early 1980s that this change was adopted (Davies 2011: 6).

The heterodox concern with the irrationality of speculation has always prevented it from appreciating the rationality of the dynamic that hides behind neoliberalism's orthodox image of money and market—that is, the generative interaction of instability and regressive risk shifting. At the very same time that capital was proving itself capable of triggering productive responses to its speculative propositions in a variety of unexpected spaces and of making value a more plastic entity than ever before, heterodox critiques became more and more concerned with separating fictitious from real value, mere form from substance. The post-Keynesian appropriation of Minsky that has come to dominate the literature sees uncertainty as an external limit to risk-based prediction, and it depicts speculation as an irrational, destabilizing practice that should be suppressed through regulation. Decrying each bailout as a hypocritical, external intervention to save speculators from themselves, it ignores the fact that Minsky saw the redistribution of liquidity constraints as an endogenous feature of the financial system itself. As Beggs (2012: 17) reminds us, the answer suggested by Minsky (1982) himself to the question "Can 'it' [i.e., the crash of 1929] happen again?" was something like "probably not," because of the level of protection embedded in the system's operation. From that angle, "the bailout and not the crisis itself might be seen as the real 'Minsky moment'" (17).

Episodes of instability and crisis are often seen as moments of sudden clarity when neoliberal capital reveals itself as lacking rational foundations and exposes its utter neglect of system risk; accordingly, they tend to be viewed as turning points or learning moments, when political institutions and communal discourses reassert themselves against the centrifugal forces of financial speculation and force a return to foundations. But such rationalist assessments tend to turn a blind eye to the often paradoxical dynamics of crisis and uncertainty. The theme of governance through Schmittian exception has achieved a degree of prominence because it speaks to the productive role of events that by most theoretically derived measures of political legitimacy should have meant the demise of neoliberalism. But we have seen some of the problems with that approach: it views crisis and instability as moments when basic normative structures disintegrate and ordinary mechanisms of ordering stop working, and the logic of exception is seen to work by deferring the state's need to legitimate itself. In this way, it insufficiently appreciates the extent to which the preemptive temporal rationality of neoliberal capitalism generates its own specific sources of legitimacy and internal cohesion.

From the perspective developed in this book, crises are more usefully seen as representing the limit case of the logic whereby neoliberalism makes uncertainty productive. Imminent failure, far from making room for arbitrary decision or external intervention, activates patterns of normalization (which can still fail to stave off failure). In such situations, even as we are entirely in the dark about the specific origins of the problem, it is often perfectly clear what must be done: we must protect the banks, the promise of the future that they hold. The interventions following the financial crisis of 2007–8, whereby the central bank became fully enlisted in supporting the balance sheets of the largest banks, mark the point where sovereignty becomes simultaneously highly speculative—investing itself in assets whose value is fundamentally in doubt—and fully driven by the normalizing logic of risk. The crisis took the form of a run on the short-term commitments of the shadow banking system (above all, repurchase agreements, or repos); when it became clear that significant amounts of bad debt were circulating in the system, confidence in shadow bank money crumbled and a "run on repo" ensued (Gorton and Metrick 2012). The panic spread in short order, and the freezing of the interbank market set in motion a fire-sale of assets that meant a contraction of balance sheets, which further restricted market liquidity (Duffie 2010). As interest rate cuts were unable to arrest the downward spiral of asset prices, the state was faced with the choice of letting markets go into a free-fall of debt deflation or sustaining asset values by declaring its willingness to absorb assets onto its books against minimum prices. Under these circumstances, the American state committed itself fully to the validation of its constitutive speculations. Greenspan's successor, Ben Bernanke, did what had to be done,[1] manifesting a paradoxical coincidence of contingency and necessity, decision and imperative.

Although this involved a series of measures without precedent that moved the Federal Reserve well beyond the Bagehot rule or any variation thereof (Hogan et al. 2015), in an important sense it was simply the expansion of the central bank's basic function. As Mehrling puts it, "the Fed was forced to put aside its inflation fine tuning and go back to basics" (2012: 107), its core activity of protecting the nodal points in the financial system. This involved lending not against good collateral but precisely against bad collateral: the only way to stop the deleveraging movement was for the American state to buy up assets at minimum prices. The bailouts represent the neoliberal logic of regressive risk socialization pushed to a spectacular extreme (Freixas 2009; Rude 2010; Mehrling 2011; Le Maux and Scialom 2013; Thompson 2013). There is of course a definite banality about the bailouts. And this has led many to discuss them as if they were external subsidies to an otherwise failing system, last-ditch attempts to keep together a financial system that has all but come undone. This book has argued against such exceptionalist understandings of central banking, and it has tried to reframe the reactionary character of bailouts as part of a more general logic of risk shifting. The bailouts can be viewed as manifesting the incoherence and unsustainable character of neoliberalism only if the deployment of public authority is assessed against an idealized conception of sovereignty, one that takes it to have transcended the economic logic of risk, speculation, and temporality.

During the following years all hoped-for measures to curtail speculation failed to materialize, and it became clear that neoliberalism had not in fact been dealt its final blow. One way in which progressively minded commentators have responded to this is by shifting political hopes from the repressive regulation of finance to regulatory concerns that already seemed to have some currency among members of the financial establishment—system risk, financial stability, and "macroprudential" governance (e.g., Bernanke 2009, 2011; Borio 2011; Haldane and May 2011; Acharya 2015).[2] On this reading, the crisis made clear that the interaction of risk exposures could jeopardize the coherence and stability of the financial system at large, and that greater attention to questions of complexity, the dynamics of failure contagion, and the design of macroprudential policies would go far in remedying the problem (Helleiner 2010; Datz 2013; Baker 2013; Casey 2015). In a very short period of time, however, this literature seems to have moved from optimistic assessments of the prospects of the postcrisis reform agenda to a concern that it has failed to make much headway (e.g., Helleiner 2014). Seen from the analysis presented in this book, the limited progressive potential of the system risk agenda should not have been all that surprising: far from being a recent discovery, the concern with system-level risk is in many ways a defining concern of central banking (Conti-Brown 2016: 150), and neoliberalism has always involved not an irrational neglect of this problematic but a distinctive way of framing it.

Currently burgeoning discourses of complexity, networks, and resilience should be seen as a series of attempts to formalize and operationalize in more precise ways what has always been a major concern of neoliberal financial governance. System risk concepts are used to study the topology of interbank networks, to assess the systemic importance of financial institutions, to understand contagion dynamics, to think about ways to deal with various forms of liquidity risk, and to model financial networks as complex systems.[3] Similarly, central banks currently devote significant resources to stress testing and scenario planning, which involves assessing system resilience under a range of statistically unlikely scenarios (Langley 2013a). It is hardly the case, then, that the implementation of the system risk management agenda has failed; it's just that it never should have been seen as signaling the transition to a postneoliberal regime in the first place. It represents above all the further development of a problematic that has always to some extent been embedded in the structures of neoliberalism (Cooper 2011; Aquanno 2015). Central bankers have tended to associate system risk thinking not primarily with outside interventions that impose restrictive regulations on the financial sector, but rather with ways to bolster the financial system's adaptive mechanisms. Techniques of system risk assessment are approached not in terms of their ability to reduce uncertainty, but precisely as a set of instruments to support and manage a distinctly neoliberal logic of financial governance that acknowledges the endogenous role of both instability and risk shifting (Levitin 2011). Concerns with system risk and financial instability have become closely allied with analyses of the procyclical dynamics of balance sheets and an awareness that the state's support for the banking system will henceforth involve the Fed's balance sheet (Adrian and Shin 2010). As Goodhart puts it, "A macro-prudential authority by itself has no money. So, it has to have access to the Central Bank's balance sheet" (2011: 103). For all practical intents and purposes of policymaking, too-big-to-fail is treated as a stabilization policy—which explains why since the crisis the American state has put little effort into preventing too-big-to-fail firms from becoming even larger and has dedicated itself above all to boosting its capacities for bailout interventions (Carstensen 2013).

The policy regime that the Federal Reserve has embarked on in recent years represents a combination of neoliberal expectations management and attention to bank balance sheets. The immediate problem the Federal Reserve faced was that it had lowered the federal funds rate to zero, so that it could no longer use this instrument for policy purposes (at least, that is, until rate increases are again called for). Under these circumstances, it adopted a policy of "quantitative easing," buying up large amounts of assets in strategically vital areas, in combination with a policy of "forward guidance" that gives the market assurances about how long the Federal Reserve will persist with its policies (Gane 2015). This situation is not in all respects new: it bears some resemblance to the way the Federal Reserve supported the market for government debt during and after World War II. But through its current programs, the Federal Reserve buys not just government debt (traditionally considered perfectly safe and secure) but also assets in areas where there is plenty of reason to doubt the value of the collateral. Quantitative easing has generally been discussed in an atmosphere that wonders when the

Federal Reserve will wind down these exceptional policies, but now that
we are a full decade beyond the crisis we may well wonder if we are not
simply witnessing adaptation rather than exception. Although the Federal Reserve has ended quantitative easing policies in the sense that it
has stopped making new purchases, there are few signs that it is ready to
sell off the assets it has accumulated on its balance sheet over the years
(and the way it will handle these investments is likely to be heavily determined by what has been the Federal Reserve's central priority during
the neoliberal era—namely, consumer price inflation). Above all, quantitative easing and forward guidance reflect the way the American state
has become fully invested in the volatile movements of the financial
system, the degree to which its capacities for governance have become
bound up with its position in a system that works on leverage, futurity,
and speculation (cf. Adam and Vines 2009).

The preoccupation with the Polanyian re-embedding movement
(that is, a repressive regulation of speculative finance) and its failure
to materialize has diverted attention from the movement that did take
place—namely the movement internal to the logic of capital, which
seeks to secure the valorization of its speculative claims. As the critics
of neoliberal finance were still wondering when the promised turn to
postneoliberal governance would commence, they were taken aback by
the emergence of a powerful austerity drive. This has been widely criticized as an irrational policy, as not simply problematic in abstract moral
terms but a massive mistake, even by capitalism's own standards. Austerity is seen as a policy, pushed by financial elites, that brings short-term
benefits to speculators while killing off prospects for the production of
real economic value (Boyer 2012; Tabb 2012; Blyth 2013; Schäfer and
Streeck 2013; Stuckler and Basu 2013; Hudson 2015). Such perspectives
suffer from many of the limitations that we have already encountered in
established critiques of neoliberalism: they connect austerity politics to
a limited set of ideas or interests and do little to trace the wider neoliberal rationality of which it is part (cf. Stanley 2014; Kiersey 2017). Such
an approach is overtly problematic in the US context, where austerity

has found considerable popular support, epitomized by its active embrace by populist Tea Party currents (Konings 2012); to them, austerity appeared as a means to restore a neutral republican market that functions as a bulwark against unearned privilege and concentrations of power.

Nor is this simply an issue of political legitimation understood in a traditional sense: neoliberalism blurs the distinction between political legitimation and economic value. Its governance techniques do not simply legitimate an already existing state of affairs but elicit a new series of investments. They do not simply provide after-the-fact rationalizations but rather invite productive responses, prompting the intensified reengagement of risk in the name of security (cf. Massumi 2014: 13). Neoliberal power works not through sidelining popular energies or immobilizing affect, but by soliciting active participation in its logic of preemption and the dialectic of speculation and austerity that functions at its heart. Recognition of the generative character of austerity has been impeded by the way the issue has quickly been analytically narrowed to one of sovereign debt, which obscures the way the austerity drive relates to question of debt, precarity, and human capital more generally. That is, the plausible argument that public fiscal austerity puts a drag on GDP growth does not consider the effects of austerity on capitalist growth in the broader sense that Foucault associated with the rise of human capital theory. It is not just that contemporary economic reason is infused with an awareness that living without debt has become a practical impossibility, but also that access to credit has never lost its association with notions of democratization and the ideal of a republican polity. The subject deemed to lack austerity is defined not by indebtedness as such, but by a hesitation to use its credit productively, by the reluctance to reorganize its commitments, attachments, and capacities in a way that will generate the resources for debt servicing. In other words, the push for austerity is driven by a spirited Hayekian critique of the character that refuses to treat its resources as capital and instead begins to criticize and question.

It is here that we can situate one of the most significant developments since the financial crisis: the accelerating expansion of student
debt (Brown 2015; Lazzarato 2015). Cutbacks in public funding for
education in recent decades have meant a drastic increase in the cost
of a university education. At the same time, various measures and laws
introduced during the neoliberal era have made it extremely difficult
to discharge student debt through the bankruptcy process. Because
of the way student debt is administered, it is far easier for lenders or
their agents to track down debtors and enforce repayment than it is
with other forms of debt. This makes the contract entered into by an
eighteen-year-old an almost sacred bond, binding in a way that no other
secular obligation is. In combination with the increasing precarity of
employment, this means that growing numbers of college graduates unable to find secure employment live a life that is permanently in danger
of falling foul of the survival constraint. It has been argued that this
represents a return to indenture (Williams 2008; Adamson 2009), but
whereas the traditional indenture contract included an employment ar-
rangement to settle the debt, the modern student loan precisely does
not come with any such guarantees. At work here is what Mitropoulos has referred to as "infinite contractualism" (2012: 27), a paradoxical
movement whereby limitless precarity becomes valorized as the speculative foundation of order (cf. Lorey 2015: 46).

These conditions place major constraints on what students can do
with the educational choices they formally enjoy. Debt-financed higher
education becomes an emblematic manifestation of the fact that "human
capital is constrained to self-invest in ways that contribute to its appreciation or at least prevent its depreciation" (Brown 2015: 177). It has entailed
a process of curricular vocationalization that has undermined the viability
of the liberal arts model, which for all its limitations and the way it was
itself deeply bound up with the reproduction of institutionalized privilege, provided some room for the development of critical faculties (Bousquet 2009). Furthermore, there is a certain kind of gratuitous ruthlessness

in the way the student debtor is treated; reports abound of repayments being enforced in overtly punitive ways that look like attempts to squeeze blood from a stone. Seen from this angle, the expanding student debt regime appears as the institutional embodiment of a Hayekian spirit of the critique of critique, as the revenge of populist-republican sentiments on the progressive character's attachment to critical knowledge, as the rejection of a subjectivity that refuses to acquire vocational skills and seeks knowledge without submitting it to the austere discipline of economy (cf. Graeber 2011).

What becomes visible here is the banal side of resilience and plasticity, a system's capacity to reproduce itself through contingency. Such notions have attracted significant interest in recent years, often accompanied by considerable optimism. This is particularly apparent in their mainstream appropriation as magical formulas for thriving under pressure and bouncing back from failure. But more critical perspectives have tended to reproduce some of these optimistic valences. For instance, Chandler (2014) argues that the rise of resilience thinking is a response to the practical failure of neoliberalism, the way continuous state interventions have put into question the belief in the efficiency of markets, and that resilience holds out the prospect of moving beyond neoliberalism. Malabou (2008) views neoliberal contingency and the imperatives of labor market flexibility that it imposes as a kind of degenerate version of the principle of plasticity, in effect suggesting that the latter not only holds out a potential for change but should be anticipated as a positive regulatory principle of a postneoliberal state. But such assessments assume that neoliberalism was entirely naïve in what it expected from the market. This book, by contrast, has argued that neoliberalism represents a more reflexive engagement with the dynamics of self-organizing processes. If it has also drawn attention to the fact that neoliberal temporality involves a highly reactionary aspect, this should by no means be taken as a reason to dismiss neoliberal notions of resilience as little more than old-fashioned ideology (e.g., Joseph 2013).

When set against the pervasive tendency to think of the production of order in primarily epistemic terms as the discursive construction of consensus and legitimacy, a Hayekian or radical-constructivist awareness of the nonrepresentational character of our practical investments, of the nonlinearity of normative structures, and of the ignorance and uncertainty that constitutively pervade the mechanisms of ordering is highly significant and politically consequential.

CHAPTER 12

Capital and Critique in Neoliberal Times

As it became apparent that the Polanyian countermovement had failed to materialize, critical scholarship became increasingly interested in the ability of neoliberalism to suspend its own contradictions and to defer its own demise (Crouch 2011; Streeck 2014). The main explanation for the failure of the reform agenda has centered on the capture of policymaking institutions and discourses by financial elites (Baker 2010; McCarty 2013; Rixen 2013; Goldbach 2015). Although this model has obvious descriptive relevance, it is less clear that it can stand on its own as an explanation: the disproportionate influence of elites on public policy is hardly a new phenomenon and in many ways it is more symptom than cause. What needs separate explanation is precisely how the wider context of financial governance has functioned so as to protect those interests at a time of intense critical scrutiny of bankers and their regulators (cf. Kiersey 2011: 25). And this is something current scholarship has little to contribute to, as it is more concerned with advancing explanations for what might have happened yet has not (the demise of neoliberalism) than with accounting for what in fact has happened (the reinvigoration of neoliberalism). Indeed, we are currently seeing the bizarre emergence of an academic growth sector devoted to explaining the failure of social reality to conform itself to social scientists' fantasies of a re-embedding movement (e.g., Helleiner 2014; Underhill 2015)—a curious imitation of the financial sector's own ability to profit from failure.

The capture model relies on an instrumentalist understanding of institutional and ideological power. In this way, the constructivist and institutionalist affinities of Polanyian theory come to be allied with crude notions of power as direct personal control and ideology as cognitive manipulation—the kind of conceptions that are routinely (and for good reason) rejected when they are advanced by Marxist scholars. The moralistic style of critique that frames the persistence of neoliberalism as exceptional, as a deviation from a model of Keynesian governance, fails to discern how a critique of exceptionalism is already a key part of neoliberal discourses. The unreflexive moment here is underlined by the neoliberal origins of capture theory; it is associated with the work of George Stigler (1971), one of the founding members of the Mont Pelerin society. Far from being a neutral analytical device, the notion of capture expresses an imaginary of corruption and purification that has always been at the heart of the neoliberal project and in particular its ability to play on anti-state sentiments to find popular traction. In this way, progressive interventions play a somewhat unthinking role in the fantasy of economic neutrality, conferring credibility on the idea of a crisis-free market economy and encouraging us to imagine a form of risk management that is not stained by the morally problematic associations of the too-big-to-fail logic. The expression of moral opprobrium within a neoliberal conceptual register means that progressive discourses have come to function above all as a rhetorical counterpoint to neoliberal discourses. The latter, in a Hayekian vein, take promises of security with a pinch of salt, deploying them especially to demand an intensified commitment to the very practices that brought on the crisis.

To borrow from Streeck's (2014) title, current policies are said to be merely buying capital time, delaying the inevitable crisis of capitalism, a system that is no longer in touch with its foundations, knows no moral limits, and is long past its objective date of expiration. This book has suggested a different take on the relation between time and capitalism, one that emphasizes their internal connections and takes seriously the way value generation engenders its own temporal structures. The provision of time is not some ultimately futile delay of an inevitable fate, but a key move in the plastic logic of value.

Yet these are hardly inauspicious times to be thinking about money and finance from an interdisciplinary perspective. Although the heterodox critique of capitalist speculation is a thriving academic industry, the fact that it claimed final vindication only several years ago means that it increasingly appears more as a moral stance than as a serious attempt to comprehend the dynamics of capitalism. Furthermore, the financial crisis has triggered an interest in economic questions and produced a degree of economic literacy among a broader public that may not be quite so easily absorbed by the conservative appeal to foundations with which the critique of speculation is associated. And although I have been critical of the way new fields such as cultural economy and social studies of finance have elaborated issues of performance and construction, there can be little doubt that they have done a great deal to stimulate new thinking on questions of economics. Of particular interest is the emergence of what has been termed "new materialism" (Coole and Frost 2010), broadly understood as a set of approaches that while retaining the critical impulses of the poststructuralist turn, rejects its tendency to rehabilitate a separation of matter and discourse. As Adkins summarizes the conceptual thrust of this new take on materialism, "we now talk regularly not of the inertness of matter, nor of external forces working *on* matter, but of the performativity of matter—of the dynamism of matter, of its very temporality" (2009: 334).

But even though such trends allow us to connect questions of topology, self-organization, and complexity to questions of value, it is not clear that the formulation of what I have termed a non-essentialist economism is particularly high on the agenda. For instance, the theme of self-organization in relation to economic processes plays a prominent role in Connolly's (2013) recent work. The world it portrays is

shaped by a multiplicity of self-organizing processes, which are nonetheless also fragile—collapse and failure is always a possibility. Economic life too has self-organizing characteristics; but it too is fragile.
Connolly views neoliberalism as a doctrine that fails to recognize or
respect the limits of economic self-organization; driven by a grandiose,
economistic belief in the self-regulating abilities of the market, it pro-
motes the self-expansion of the market at the expense of the pluralism
that a livable universe requires. Here is more than a faint Polanyian
echo of an undertheorized self-expansionary dynamic in combination
with a pluralist idealism. A similar logic seems to be at work in Latour's
(2013) recent work. The tragedy of the moderns is that even as they
have constructed so many things so well, they have become stuck in
critical sentiment, unhelpfully invested in the imagined purity of their
constructions. Latour enjoins and anticipates a politics of assemblage
that is purely pragmatic and instrumental, regulated by a diplomatic
ethos that is affirmative and moves beyond critique. But although the
conceits and confusions of modernity can be found in any domain of
life, it appears that for Latour it is really the reach of capital that stops
such a pluralist politics from materializing, preventing us from moving from an economy that is increasingly "uninhabitable" (2013: 23) to
an ecology of multiple orders of value.[1] What is not explained is what
makes the economy so dangerous, prone to excessive, predatory expansion in a way that other spheres are not. It is especially when seen in this
context that the appeal to diplomacy as a means to negotiate differences
comes to seem somewhat naïve, and that it becomes difficult to see how
Latour's conceptual schema is more than a watered-down version of
Habermasian discourse ethics.

   The aims of the new materialism are of course not altogether different from the original ambitions of actor-network theory (indeed,
Latour is the figure of continuity here)—that is, to move beyond the
stale opposition of materialism and idealism and to formulate a "material semiotics." We have seen how actor-network theory sought to
settle this issue prematurely and as a result has tended to get caught in

an unstable back-and-forth between materialism and idealism. Many of
the authors working in the new materialism are more directly engaged
with the ways poststructuralist critiques of materialism and economism
have tended to reproduce their own idealist brand of essentialism. But
the heightened awareness of how thorny the problem truly is does not
by itself offer any guarantees for avoiding a similar fate. Drawing on
Luhmann, this book has proposed that we can only hope to avoid a
back-and-forth between materialism and idealism by thematizing our
own inability to resolve this issue and by foregrounding the paradoxes
of self-referentiality. And it has connected this to the question of the
self-referential character of money and the self-expansionary tendencies
of financial capital. In this way, the book has tried to rework the Marxist critique of capitalism along non-essentialist lines, relying on one of
the most modest impulses in the contemporary social sciences to begin
rescaffolding a radical critique.

Latour's preoccupation with an affirmative politics is driven by a
concern that the critical project has had its day (Latour 2004). But the
way his own work circles back onto a Polanyian format and takes on
its own kind of moralistic qualities suggests that the project of critique
cannot be so cavalierly left behind, and that we should be careful not to
let the rejection of foundationalist critique become the excuse for a loss
of interest in generating critical resources altogether. Like Latour, Luhmann rejects the kind of critical theory that seeks an external vantage
point, the self-satisfied critique of others' mistaken beliefs that imagines
itself as occupying a view from nowhere. But he would no doubt have
rejected Latour's claims for the affirmative powers of the critique of
critique as itself a kind of faux radicalism, perhaps even noting its odd
similarity to the Hayekian spirit of neoliberal capitalism. From a Luhmannian angle, the ambition to move beyond critique appears as an
arbitrary, self-imposed constraint on our observations. Although we can
never observe our world from the outside, we can always generate new
observations that allow us to see new things. Just as it is not possible
to move beyond misrecognition, confusion, and ignorance, so it is not

possible to move beyond critique. This is not to say that no qualitative differences exist between uncritical and critical knowledge, but rather that it is not possible to provide an objective set of criteria for what makes knowledge critical. A good critique is a performative achievement; we recognize it when we encounter it. Thinking about why a critique is successful may be very useful in developing our critical faculties, but it never generates an external standard for critical knowledge. To ask more of critique than such resonant performances (for instance, "What is to be done?") is to confer on it a responsibility it is poorly equipped to handle, and to tempt it down the path of one foundationalism or another.

Acknowledgments

For useful comments and insightful conversations that helped me to formulate the ideas in this book, I would like to thank the following: Melinda Cooper, Gavin Fridell, Dick Bryan, Damien Cahill, Fiona Allon, Mike Beggs, Mike Rafferty, Adam Morton, Samuel Knafo, Amin Samman, Ronen Palan, Lisa Adkins, Elena Esposito, Nina Boy, Ute Tellmann, Marieke de Goede, Stefano Sgambati, Leigh Claire La Berge, Carey Hardin, Bob Meister, Ed LiPuma, and Ben Lee. I worked on this book while I was a visiting scholar at New York University, and I would like to thank Arjun Appadurai and Robert Wosnitzer for their help in arranging my appointment. Perry Mehrling and Nick Gane reviewed the manuscript for Stanford University Press and I am grateful for their perceptive readings.

Working with Emily-Jane Cohen has again been a real pleasure: I am grateful for her generous support of my work and her unmatched editorial insight, as well as for her interest in setting up the series in which this book appears. My thanks also to Anne Fuzellier for her help with the production process, and to Jeff Wyneken for his meticulous copyediting of the manuscript.

I gratefully acknowledge the financial support of the Australian Research Council under grant number DE120100213.

Bhavani let me work on this book and put up with my writing quirks during a particularly hectic time. It took me as long to write this book as it took Anik to grow from a juicy dumpling into a kind and confident little guy. This is neither the book about carrots nor the book about people and cars that he would have liked to see, but I expect it will spark engaged conversations and inspired soliloquys all the same.

Notes

Introduction

1. Although he is more specifically concerned with the ethos of financial trading, Appadurai defines the contemporary approach to the uses of uncertainty in a similar way:

> I propose that the primary feature of the ethos of financial players in the past few decades, those who have both played and shaped the financial game, is to be found in a working (though not consciously theorized or articulated) disposition toward exploiting uncertainty as a legitimate principle for managing risk. In other words, those players who define the strategies through which financial devices are developed and operated (as opposed to those who simply react or comply with these strategies) use their own intuitions, experiences, and sense of the moment to outplay other players who might be excessively dominated by their tools for handling risk alone. (2011: 525)

2. As Brown explains the concept of neoliberal rationality:

> "Political rationality" or "governing rationality" are the terms Foucault used for apprehending, among other things, the way that neoliberalism comes to govern as a normative form of reason. . . . political actions, regimes, violence, and everyday practices ought neither to be understood as simply emanating from the intentions of rulers or participants nor, on the other hand, as driven by either material conditions or ideology. Rather, he uses the term "political rationality" to identify the governing form of normative reason that, as Mitchell Dean formulates it, is both "anterior to political action and a condition of it." (2015: 115)

Chapter 1

1. We might also note here the intellectual trajectory of Wolfgang Streeck, who spent most of his career as a Keynesian-institutionalist political economist but has in recent years emerged as one of the most visible and outspoken

left-wing critics of neoliberal capitalism. Radicalized by the failure of elites to respond appropriately to the financial crisis, he draws in his current work (2014) on both Polanyian theory and Frankfurt School theory (which in earlier years he had found too abstract and formalistic to be of much interest to the analysis of real-world capitalism).

2. For authoritative anthologies in the fields of economic sociology and international political economy, see Granovetter and Swedberg (2011); and Blyth (2009).

Chapter 3

1. See also Shackle's comment that a norm or convention is nothing but "that spontaneous coalescing of thought which is so powerfully fostered by the very absence of 'real' clues to the future" (1972: 193).

Chapter 4

1. See Shackle (1972: 217–18) on the two faces of Keynes's *General Theory*.

2. Such an approach is more useful than following Luhmann's own take on the governance problems of the postwar order, which revolved around the idea that the balance between different subsystems had been thrown out of sync. This at times made his position difficult to distinguish from Habermasian diagnoses of the difficulties experienced by Western welfare states (Borch 2011: 120–21).

Chapter 5

1. Of considerable importance here is the influence of Canguilhem's work, which advances an understanding of living systems as constructing their own normative structures through "the polarity between two tendencies, self-regulation and self-transgression" (Muhle 2014: 95).

Chapter 6

1. Traditionally, the malleability of values was registered by combining the balance sheet with an income statement, which shows profits and losses and thus the increase or decrease in the value of capital (which can then be updated on the balance sheet itself). Nowadays, mark-to-market accounting means that changes in values are directly and continuously visible on the balance sheet itself (Levy 2014: 209).

Chapter 7

1. Contributions that concentrate on the logic of the derivative have emphasized the difficulty of making clear distinctions between hedging and speculative financing (Bryan and Rafferty 2006; Engel 2013; Lee and Martin 2016).

Risk avoidance and security become themselves speculative propositions, requiring the continuous differentiation of financial positions. Shackle's comments on the spurious distinction between the transactions motive and speculative motive are also germane in this context:

> The transactions motive and the speculative motive may, by the appeal to their common source in lack of knowledge, be shown to be essentially the same. In all but this basic origin they appear perhaps very different. Yet they have one further character in common. In both, the boundary is blurred between defence and attack, between avoidance of loss and the making of profit, between safety and success. This is in the nature of things. Those theories, in any part of the field of economic phenomena, which make a sharp distinction between profitability, on one hand, and safety, or power of survival, on the other, are evidently neglecting uncertainty. (1972: 215)

2. This phrase, suggesting as it does the essential self-referentiality of the financial system, would also be an excellent summary of the core idea of Luhmann's *Wirtschaft der Gesellschaft* (1988). Although Luhmann's engagement with economics was limited for reasons discussed in the previous chapter, his systems-theoretical take on economic life did allow him to recognize the (interbank) payments system as the nervous system of contemporary capitalism, to appreciate that payment failure is not a discrete event but can have dramatic knock-on effects, and to situate the main imperatives of central banking with respect to these conditions (1988, 2002a: 182).

3. As Ricks puts it, "The issuance of large quantities of money-claims that are continuously rolled over is the defining feature of our concept of banking" (2016: 52).

4. Hedge financing refers to a balance sheet structure where current revenues arising from an investment are sufficient to cover the cash commitments (payments on both principal and interest) entailed by the debt used to finance the asset. In a speculative financing structure, current revenues cover the interest payments but are insufficient to pay down the principal, and so the ability to maintain this speculative structure depends on the possibility of rolling over debt. In Ponzi finance, projected cash flows are not enough even to meet interest payments and a Ponzi unit will therefore need to borrow just for this purpose. The more speculative a position is, the more the ability to maintain payments becomes dependent on wider market dynamics—that is, on the continued appreciation of the asset bought. See Minsky (1977).

5. To put this point differently, there is a tension within post-Keynesian theory between claims regarding the endogeneity of money—as arising out of dynamics of credit and debt, which suggests that order does not preexist speculation—and the idea that speculative financing practices are in and of themselves destabilizing.

Chapter 8

1. "Construction of standard economic theory—the neoclassical synthesis—starts by examining bartering, such as might take place at a village fair, and proceeds by adding production, capital assets, money, and financial assets to the basic model. Such a village fair paradigm shows that a decentralized market mechanism can lead to a coherent result" (Minsky 1982: 61). Shackle usefully states the point at somewhat greater length:

> The more nearly the economic society is confined to a hand-to-mouth existence, the more nearly, in principle, can its operations approach the rational. For when the goods dealt in on the markets are perishable and ephemeral, they must be exchanged at once and therefore find a price at once, and there will be no considerations bearing on that price except the immediate needs, tastes and momentary endowments of the members of a society. Prices in such a society must be formed; they can be formed because they are properly based on definite and simple data. It is the introduction of "wealth," of assets which promise and represent permanence or persistence, that must destroy the basis of rationality. (Shackle 1972: 157–58)

Investments get us entangled with others in a way that momentary, individual acts of consumption do not, and we can never be quite sure about how they will respond.

2. In Smith's own words:

> When a bank discounts to a merchant a real bill of exchange drawn by a real creditor upon a real debtor, and which, as soon as it becomes due, is really paid by that debtor, it only advances to him a part of the value which he would otherwise be obliged to keep by him unemployed and in ready money for answering occasional demands. The payment of the bill, when it becomes due, replaces to the bank the value of what it had advanced, together with the interest. The coffers of the bank, so far as its dealings are confined to such customers, resemble a water pond, from which, though a stream is continually running out, yet another is continually running in, fully equal to that which runs out. (1999 [1776]: 402)

3. This relates to the much-debated question of whether the political commitments of Scottish Enlightenment thinkers such as Hume and Smith should be understood as primarily liberal or republican. As Kalyvas and Katznelson (2008) point out, this issue is very difficult to resolve on the basis of textual evidence, and they argue a need to recognize that during the late eighteenth and early nineteenth century liberalism and republicanism were simply not clearly differentiated (see also MacGilvray 2011). But by associating liberalism primarily with claims about the utilitarian efficiency of free exchange, and re-

publicanism with intersubjective sympathies conducive to egalitarian forms of community, Kalyvas and Katznelson nonetheless reproduce the distinction in their own way (cf. Pangle 1988: 30; Jurdjevic 2001). By associating republican values specifically with non-economic factors, they are unable to appreciate that there is something about the concept of market neutrality itself, in its distinctly modern economic sense, that has a certain utopian quality, a strong intuitive appeal. As a consequence they are unable to trace how republican sentiments nowadays *still* play a key role in the capitalist imaginary, and how neoliberalism has capitalized on this.

4. Thornton was dismissive of the tendency to be alarmed by the mere growth of credit money—"Paper constitutes, it is true, an article on the credit side of the books of some men; but it forms an exactly equal item on the debit side of the books of others" (1965 [1802]: 79). For him, all interesting questions had to do with the specific dynamics generated by this relational character of money.

5. On these debates, see Viner (1937), Morgan (1943), and Mints (1945).

Chapter 9

1. Mehrling explains Minsky's take on the inflation of the 1970s as follows: "inflation continually boosted cash flows beyond what they were expected to be, and so made it possible to meet debt commitments de jure if not de facto because payments were made in depreciated currency. The effect was as if, instead of some fraction of debtors defaulting completely, all debtors defaulted partially" (1999: 147).

Chapter 10

1. Indeed, he is explicitly critical of Schmitt's decisionist disdain for the rule of law (Hayek 1973: 71).

2. At times, this injunction to accept the past without questioning gives Hayek's thinking a somewhat banal flavor: the profundity of his insights into plasticity and system self-organization such as those offered in *The Sensory Order* (1952) is surpassed only by the banality of his dismissal of social justice as an empty and nonsensical concept merely on the grounds that society is not planned by a single transcendental mind (in such passages Hayek sounds more like a member of the Vienna Circle than the Austrian school of economics) (1976b: 62–85).

3. At various points in *Law, Legislation and Liberty* (1973–79) Hayek simply stresses the importance of an independent central bank that secures a stable, noninflationary currency, without ever considering the specific modalities of money production and the basic mechanisms of financial policymaking.

Chapter 11

1. "Making politically unpopular decisions for the long-run benefit of the country is the reason the Fed exists as a politically independent central bank. It was created for precisely this purpose: to do what must be done—what others cannot or will not do" (Bernanke 2015: xiii).

2. Macroprudential governance is to be contrasted with a "microprudential" approach that supposedly prevailed before the crisis; whereas the latter assesses the health of financial institutions on an individual basis, the former takes into account the linkages among financial institutions.

3. For a representative sample of what is already a massive literature, see Bech and Atalay (2010), Anand et al. (2012), Anand et al. (2013), Bougheas and Kirman (2014), Hüser (2015), and Levy-Carciente et al. (2015).

Chapter 12

1. "By identifying technological innovations (TEC), the splendors of works of art (FIC), the objectivity of the sciences (REF), political autonomy (POL), respect for legal linkages (LAW), the appeal of the living God (REL), [the Moderns] would have glowed in the world like one of the most beautiful, most durable, most fruitful civilizations of all. Proud of themselves, they would have had no burden weighing them down, crushing them like Atlas, like Sisyphus, like Prometheus, all those tragic giants. But they went on to invent something else: the continent of *The Economy*" (Latour 2013: 379). Or as he puts it elsewhere, the economy is "an infinite and boundless domain totally indifferent to terrestrial existence and the very notion of limits, and entirely self-centered and self-governed" (2014: 6).

Bibliography

Abdelal, Rawi. 2009. "Constructivism as an Approach to International Political Economy." In *Routledge Handbook of International Political Economy (IPE)*, edited by Mark Blyth, 62–76. London: Routledge.

Abdelal, Rawi, Mark Blyth, and Craig Parsons, eds. 2010. *Constructing the International Economy*. Ithaca: Cornell University Press.

Abdelal, Rawi, Yoshiko M. Herrera, Alastair Iain Johnston, and Rose McDermott, eds. 2009. *Measuring Identity: A Guide for Social Scientists*. Cambridge: Cambridge University Press.

Acharya, Viral. 2015. "Financial Stability in the Broader Mandate for Central Banks: A Political Economy Perspective." Brookings, Hutchins Center Working Paper no. 11.

Adam, Barbara. 1990. *Time and Social Theory*. Cambridge: Polity.

Adam, Christopher, and David Vines. 2009. "Remaking Macroeconomic Policy after the Global Financial Crisis: A Balance-Sheet Approach." *Oxford Review of Economic Policy* 25 (4): 507–552.

Adams, Vincanne, Michelle Murphy, and Adele E. Clarke. 2009. "Anticipation: Technoscience, Life, Affect, Temporality." *Subjectivity* 28 (1): 246–265.

Adamson, Morgan. 2009. "The Human Capital Strategy." *ephemera* 9 (4): 271–284.

Adey, Peter, Ben Anderson, and Stephen Graham. 2015. "Introduction: Governing Emergencies: Beyond Exceptionality." *Theory, Culture and Society* 32 (2): 3–17.

Adkins, Lisa. 2009. "Feminism after Measure." *Feminist Theory* 10 (3): 323–339.

———. 2012. "Out of Work or out of Time? Rethinking Labor after the Financial Crisis." *South Atlantic Quarterly* 111 (4): 621–641.

Adkins, Lisa, and Celia Lury. 2011. "Introduction: Special Measures." *Sociological Review* 59 (s2): 5–23.

Adrian, Tobias, and Hyun Song Shin. 2010. "Liquidity and Leverage." *Journal of Financial Intermediation* 19 (3): 418–437.

Agamben, Giorgio. 1998. *Homo Sacer: Sovereign Power and Bare Life*. Stanford: Stanford University Press.

———. 2005. *State of Exception*. Chicago: University of Chicago Press.

———. 2011. *The Kingdom and the Glory: For a Theological Genealogy of Economy and Government*. Stanford: Stanford University Press.

Aglietta, Michel, and Laurence Scialom. 2008. "Permanence and Innovation in Central Banking Policy for Financial Stability." Economix Working Paper 2008-21.

Aitken, Rob. 2007. *Performing Capital: Toward a Cultural Economy of Popular and Global Finance*. Basingstoke: Palgrave Macmillan.

Allen, Thomas M. 2008. *A Republic in Time: Temporality and Social Imagination in Nineteenth-Century America*. Chapel Hill: University of North Carolina Press.

Alliez, Eric. 1996. *Capital Times: Tales from the Conquest of Time*. Minneapolis: University of Minnesota Press.

Allon, Fiona. 2015. "Everyday Leverage, or Leveraging the Everyday." *Cultural Studies* 29 (5–6): 687–706.

Amoore, Louise. 2013. *The Politics of Possibility*. Durham: Duke University Press.

Anand, Kartik, Prasanna Gai, Sujit Kapadia, Simon Brennan, and Matthew Willison. 2013. "A Network Model of Financial System Resilience." *Journal of Economic Behavior and Organization* 85: 219–235.

Anand, Kartik, Prasanna Gai, and Matteo Marsili. 2012. "Rollover Risk, Network Structure and Systemic Financial Crises." *Journal of Economic Dynamics and Control* 36 (8): 1088–1100.

Anderson, Ben. 2010. "Preemption, Precaution, Preparedness: Anticipatory Action and Future Geographies." *Progress in Human Geography* 34 (6): 777–798.

Angelis, Massimo de, and David Harvie. 2009. "'Cognitive Capitalism' and the Rat-Race: How Capital Measures Immaterial Labour in British Universities." *Historical Materialism* 17 (3): 3–30.

Appadurai, Arjun. 2011. "The Ghost in the Financial Machine." *Public Culture* 23 (3): 517–539.

———. 2015. *Banking on Words: The Failure of Language in the Age of Derivative Finance*. Chicago: University of Chicago Press.

Aquanno, Scott M. 2015. "Crisis, Continuity and Learning: The Institutional Origins of Subprime Management at the Federal Reserve." *Competition and Change* 19 (1): 3–18.

Arnon, Arie. 2011. *Monetary Theory and Policy from Hume and Smith to Wicksell: Money, Credit and the Economy*. Cambridge: Cambridge University Press.

Arvidsson, Adam. 2009. "The Ethical Economy: Towards a Post-capitalist Theory of Value." *Capital and Class* 33 (1): 13–29.

————. 2011. "General Sentiment: How Value and Affect Converge in the Information Economy." *Sociological Review* 59 (s2): 39–59.

Ascher, Ivan. 2016. *Portfolio Society: On the Capitalist Mode of Prediction*. Brooklyn: Zone Books.

Ashton, Philip. 2011. "The Financial Exception and the Reconfiguration of Credit Risk in US Mortgage Markets." *Environment and Planning A* 43 (8): 1796–1812.

Asso, Pier Francesco, George A. Kahn, and Robert Leeson. 2007. "The Taylor Rule and the Transformation of Monetary Policy." Federal Reserve Bank of Kansas City Research Working Papers 07-11.

Athavale, Manoj. 2000. "Uninsured Deposits and the Too-Big-to-Fail Policy in 1984 and 1991." *American Business Review* 18 (2): 123–128.

Atkinson, G., and Ch. Whalen. 2011. "Futurity: Cornerstone of Post-Keynesian Institutionalism." In *Financial Instability and Economy Security after the Great Recession*, edited by C. Whalen, 53–74. Cheltenham: Edward Elgar.

Axilrod, Stephen H. 2011. *Inside the Fed: Monetary Policy and Its Management, Martin through Greenspan to Bernanke*. Cambridge: MIT Press.

Ayache, Elie. 2010. *The Blank Swan: The End of Probability*. Chichester: Wiley.

Baecker, Dirk. 1991. *Womit handeln Banken? Eine Untersuchung zur Risikoverarbeitung in der Wirtschaft*. Frankfurt am Main: Suhrkamp.

Baert, Patrick. 1992. *Time, Self and Social Being: Temporality within a Sociological Context*. Aldershot: Avebury.

Bagehot, Walter. 1962 [1873]. *Lombard Street: A Description of the Money Market*. Westport: Hyperion Press.

Baker, Andrew. 2010. "Restraining Regulatory Capture? Anglo-America, Crisis Politics and Trajectories of Change in Global Financial Governance." *International Affairs* 86 (3): 647–663.

————. 2013. "The New Political Economy of the Macroprudential Ideational Shift." *New Political Economy* 18 (1): 112–139.

Baker, Dean. 2009. *Plunder and Blunder: The Rise and Fall of the Bubble Economy*. Sausalito: PoliPointPress.

Barba, Aldo, and Massimo Pivetti. 2009. "Rising Household Debt: Its Causes and Macroeconomic Implications: A Long-Period Analysis." *Cambridge Journal of Economics* 33 (1): 113–137.

Baring, Sir Francis. 1967 [1797]. *Observations on the Establishment of the Bank of England and on the Paper Circulation of the Country*. New York: A. M. Kelley.

Bech, Morten L., and Enghin Atalay. 2010. "The Topology of the Federal Funds Market." *Physica A: Statistical Mechanics and Its Applications* 389 (22): 5223–5246.

Becker, Gary S. 1964. *Human Capital: A Theoretical and Empirical Analysis, with Special Reference to Education*. Chicago: University of Chicago Press.

Beckert, Jens. 2016. *Imagined Futures: Fictional Expectations and Capitalist Dynamics*. Princeton: Princeton University Press.

Beggs, Mike. 2012. "Liquidity as a Social Relation." Paper presented to the Eastern Economic Association Conference, Boston, March 9–10.

Bell, Stephanie. 2001. "The Role of the State and the Hierarchy of Money." *Cambridge Journal of Economics* 25 (2): 149–163.

Bell, Stephen, and John Quiggin. 2006. "Asset Price Instability and Policy Responses: The Legacy of Liberalization." *Journal of Economic Issues* 40 (3): 629–649.

Bernanke, Ben S. 2009. "Financial Reform to Address Systemic Risk." Council on Foreign Relations, Washington, DC, March 10.

———. 2011. "Implementing a Macroprudential Approach to Supervision and Regulation." Forty-Seventh Annual Conference on Bank Structure and Competition, Chicago, May 5.

———. 2015. *The Courage to Act: A Memoir of a Crisis and Its Aftermath*. New York: Norton.

Bernanke, Ben S., and Mark Gertler. 1999. "Monetary Policy and Asset Volatility." *Federal Reserve Bank of Kansas City Economic Review* 84: 417–452.

———. 2001. "Should Central Banks Respond to Movements in Asset Prices?" *American Economic Review* 91 (2): 253–257.

Bignon, Vincent, Marc Flandreau, and Stefano Ugolini. 2012. "Bagehot for Beginners: The Making of Lending of Last Resort Operations in the Mid-19th Century." *Economic History Review* 65 (2): 580–608.

Blinder, Alan S., and Ricardo Reis. 2005. "Understanding the Greenspan Standard." Center for Economic Policy Studies Working Paper no. 114, www.princeton.edu/ceps/workingpapers/114blinderreis.pdf.

Block, Fred, and Margaret R. Somers. 2014. *The Power of Market Fundamentalism: Karl Polanyi's Critique*. Cambridge: Harvard University Press.

Blyth, Mark. 2002. *Great Transformations: Economic Ideas and Institutional Change in the Twentieth Century*. New York: Cambridge University Press.

———. 2003. "Structures Do Not Come with an Instruction Sheet: Interests, Ideas, and Progress in Political Science." *Perspectives on Politics* 1 (4): 695–706.

———. 2009. *Routledge Handbook of International Political Economy (IPE): IPE as a Global Conversation*. Abingdon: Routledge.

———. 2013. *Austerity: The History of a Dangerous Idea*. Oxford: Oxford University Press.

Board of Governors of the Federal Reserve System. 2017. "Historical Data, Consumer Credit Outstanding," www.federalreserve.gov/releases/g19/HIST/cc_hist_sa_levels.html.

Böhm, S., and C. Land. 2009. "No Measure for Culture? Value in the New Economy." *Capital and Class* 33 (1): 75–98.

Bonefeld, Werner. 2012. "Freedom and the Strong State: On German Ordoliberalism." *New Political Economy* 17 (5): 633–656.

Borch, Christian. 2011. *Niklas Luhmann.* New York: Routledge.

Borio, Claudio. 2011. "Implementing a Macroprudential Framework: Blending Boldness and Realism." *Capitalism and Society* 6 (1): 1–23.

Bougheas, Spiros, and Alan P. Kirman. 2014. "Complex Financial Networks and Systemic Risk: A Review." CESifo Working Paper no. 4756.

Bousquet, Marc. 2009. "Take Your Ritalin and Shut Up." *South Atlantic Quarterly* 108 (4): 623–649.

Boyer, Robert. 2012. "The Four Fallacies of Contemporary Austerity Policies: The Lost Keynesian Legacy." *Cambridge Journal of Economics* 36 (1): 283–312.

Braidotti, Rosi. 2007. "Bio-power and Necro-politics." *Springerin* 7 (2): 18–23.

Bremner, Robert P. 2004. *Chairman of the Fed: William McChesney Martin Jr., and the Creation of the Modern American Financial System.* New Haven: Yale University Press.

Brown, Wendy. 2003. "Neo-liberalism and the End of Liberal Democracy." *Theory and Event* 7 (1).

———. 2015. *Undoing the Demos: Neoliberalism's Stealth Revolution.* New York: Zone.

Bryan, Dick. 2012. "Going Forward: The Perpetual Crisis of Finance." *Culture and Organization* 18 (2): 171–176.

Bryan, Dick, Randy Martin, Johnna Montgomerie, and Karel Williams. 2012. "An Important Failure: Knowledge Limits and the Financial Crisis." *Economy and Society* 41 (3): 299–315.

Bryan, Dick, and Michael Rafferty. 2006. *Capitalism with Derivatives. A Political Economy of Financial Derivatives, Capital and Class.* Houndmills: Palgrave Macmillan.

———. 2013. "Fundamental Value: A Category in Transformation." *Economy and Society* 42 (1): 130–153.

Bucher, Bernd. 2014. "Acting Abstractions: Metaphors, Narrative Structures, and the Eclipse of Agency." *European Journal of International Relations* 20 (3): 742–765.

Buck-Morss, Susan. 2007. "Visual Empire." *diacritics* 37 (2–3): 171–198.

Burns, Arthur F. 1979. "The Anguish of Central Banking." 1979 Per Jacobsson Lecture.

Butler, Judith. 2010. "Performative Agency." *Journal of Cultural Economy* 3 (2): 147–161.

Butos, William N., and Roger G. Koppl. 1997. "The Varieties of Subjectivism: Keynes and Hayek on Expectations." *History of Political Economy* 29 (2): 327–359.

Caffentzis, George. 2005. "Immeasurable Value? An Essay on Marx's Legacy." *the commonor* (10): 87–114.

Cahill, Damien. 2014. *The End of Laissez-Faire? On the Durability of Embedded Neoliberalism*. Cheltenham: Edward Elgar.

Calder, Lendol. 1999. *Financing the American Dream: A Cultural History of Consumer Credit*. Princeton: Princeton University Press.

Caldwell, Bruce. 2004. *Hayek's Challenge: An Intellectual Biography of F.A. Hayek*. Chicago: University of Chicago Press.

Callon, M., Y. Millo, and F. Muniesa, eds. 2007. *Market Devices*. Oxford: Blackwell.

Callon, Michel. 1986. "Some Elements of a Sociology of Translation: Domestication of the Scallops and the Fishermen of St Brieuc Bay." In *Power, Action and Belief: A New Sociology of Knowledge*, edited by John Law, 196–233. London: Routledge.

———. 1991. "Techno-economic Networks and Irreversibility." In *A Sociology of Monsters: Essays on Power, Technology and Domination*, edited by John Law, 132–161. London: Routledge.

———. 1998. "Introduction: The Embeddedness of Economic Markets in Economics." In *The Laws of the Markets*, edited by Michel Callon, 1–57. Oxford: Blackwell.

———. 2007. "What Does It Mean to Say That Economics Is Performative?" In *Do Economists Make Markets? On the Performativity of Economics*, edited by Donald MacKenzie, Fabian Muniesa, and Lucia Siu, 311–357. Princeton: Princeton University Press.

Calomiris, Charles W., and Joseph R. Mason. 2003. "Fundamentals, Panics, and Bank Distress during the Depression." *American Economic Review* 93 (5): 1615–1647.

Cameron, Gregory. 2008. "Oikos and Economy: The Greek Legacy in Economic Thought." *PhaenEx* 3 (1): 112–133.

Carruthers, Bruce G., and Wendy Nelson Espeland. 1991. "Accounting for Rationality: Double-Entry Bookkeeping and the Rhetoric of Economic Rationality." *American Journal of Sociology* 97 (1): 31–69.

Carstensen, Martin B. 2013. "Bailout by Stealth? Special Bank Resolution Regimes, State Capacity and the Problem of 'Too Big to Fail'." Paper presented at the International Studies Association Annual Convention, San Francisco, April 3–6, 2013.

Casey, Terrence. 2015. "How Macroprudential Financial Regulation Can Save Neoliberalism." *British Journal of Politics and International Relations* 17 (2): 351–370.

Castel, Robert. 2003. *From Manual Workers to Wage Laborers: Transformation of the Social Question.* New Brunswick: Transaction.

Cecchetti, Stephen G., and Piti Disyatat. 2010. "Central Bank Tools and Liquidity Shortages." *Federal Reserve Bank of New York Economic Policy Review* (August): 29–42.

Chandler, David. 2014. "Beyond Neoliberalism: Resilience, the New Art of Governing Complexity." *Resilience: International Policies, Practices and Discourses* 2 (1): 47–63.

Cilliers, Paul. 1998. *Complexity and Postmodernism.* London: Routledge.

———. 2001. "Boundaries, Hierarchies and Networks in Complex Systems." *International Journal of Innovation Management* 5 (2): 135–147.

Clam, Jean. 2000. "System's Sole Constituent, the Operation: Clarifying a Central Concept of Luhmannian Theory." *Acta Sociologica* 43: 63–79.

Clarke, Simon. 1982. *Marx, Marginalism and Modern Sociology: From Adam Smith to Max Weber.* London: Macmillan.

———. 1988. *Keynesianism, Monetarism and the Crisis of the State.* Cheltenham: Edward Elgar.

Clough, Patricia Ticineto, Greg Goldberg, Rachel Schiff, Aaron Weeks, and Craig Willse. 2007. "Notes Towards a Theory of Affect-Itself." *ephemera* 7 (1): 60–77.

Cohan, William D. 2010. *House of Cards: A Tale of Hubris and Wretched Excess on Wall Street.* New York: Anchor.

Connolly, William E. 2005. *Pluralism.* Durham: Duke University Press.

———. 2013. *The Fragility of Things: Self-Organizing Processes, Neoliberal Fantasies, and Democratic Activism.* Durham: Duke University Press.

Conti-Brown, Peter. 2016. *The Power and Independence of the Federal Reserve.* Princeton: Princeton University Press.

Coole, Diana, and Samantha Frost, eds. 2010. *New Materialisms: Ontology, Agency, and Politics.* Durham: Duke University Press.

Cooper, Melinda. 2006. "Pre-empting Emergence: The Biological Turn in the War on Terror." *Theory, Culture and Society* 23 (4): 113–135.

———. 2008. *Life as Surplus: Biotechnology and Capitalism in the Neoliberal Era.* Seattle: University of Washington Press.

———. 2011. "Complexity Theory after the Financial Crisis." *Journal of Cultural Economy* 4 (4): 371–385.

———. 2015. "Shadow Money and the Shadow Workforce: Rethinking Labor and Liquidity." *South Atlantic Quarterly* 114 (2): 395–423.

Cooper, Melinda, and Martijn Konings. 2015. "Contingency and Foundation: Rethinking Money, Debt and Finance after the Crisis." *South Atlantic Quarterly* 114 (2): 239–250.

Cristi, F. R. 1984. "Hayek and Schmitt on the Rule of Law." *Canadian Journal of Political Science* 17 (3): 521–535.

Critchley, Simon. 2007. *Infinitely Demanding: Ethics of Commitment, Politics of Resistance*. London: Verso.

Crouch, Colin. 2011. *The Strange Non-death of Neo-liberalism*. Cambridge: Polity.

Dale, Gareth. 2010. *Karl Polanyi: The Limits of the Market*. Cambridge: Polity.

Dardot, Pierre, and Christian Laval. 2014. *The New Way of the World: On Neoliberal Society*. London: Verso.

Datz, Giselle. 2013. "The Narrative of Complexity in the Crisis of Finance: Epistemological Challenge and Macroprudential Policy Response." *New Political Economy* 18 (4): 459–479.

Davidson, Paul. 1991. "Is Probability Theory Relevant for Uncertainty? A Post Keynesian Perspective." *Journal of Economic Perspectives* 5 (1): 129–143.

———. 2006. "Keynes and Money." In *A Handbook of Alternative Monetary Economics*, edited by Philip Arestis and Malcolm C. Sawyer, 139–153. Cheltenham: Edward Elgar.

Davies, Phil. 2011. "Taking the Measure of Prices and Inflation." *The Region* 25 (4): 28–38.

Davies, William, and Linsey McGoey. 2012. "Rationalities of Ignorance: On Financial Crisis and the Ambivalence of Neo-liberal Epistemology." *Economy and Society* 41 (1): 64–83.

Dean, Mitchell. 1999. *Governmentality: Power and Rule in Modern Society*. London: Sage.

Degen, Robert A. 1987. *The American Monetary System: A Concise Survey of Its Evolution since 1896*. Toronto: Lexington.

Deleuze, Gilles. 1986. *Nietzsche and Philosophy*. New York: Continuum.

Desan, Christine. 2015. *Making Money: Coin, Currency, and the Coming of Capitalism*. Oxford: Oxford University Press.

Deutschmann, Christoph. 1999. *Die Verheißung des absoluten Reichtums*. Frankfurt: Campus.

———. 2011. "A Pragmatist Theory of Capitalism." *Socioeconomic Review* 9 (1): 83–106.

———. 2015. "Disembedded Markets as a Mirror of Society: Blind Spots of Social Theory." *European Journal of Social Theory* 18 (4): 368–389.

Dillon, Michael. 2008. "Underwriting Security." *Security Dialogue* 39 (2–3): 309–332.

Duffie, Darrell. 2010. *How Big Banks Fail: And What to Do about It*. Princeton: Princeton University Press.

Duncan, Richard. 2012. *The New Depression: The Breakdown of the Paper Money Economy*. Singapore: Wiley.

Düppe, Till. 2011. *The Making of the Economy: A Phenomenology of Economic Science*. Lanham: Lexington.

Durand, Cédric. 2017. *Fictitious Capital: How Finance Is Appropriating Our Future*. London: Verso.

Elson, Diane. 1979. "The Value Theory of Labour." In *Value: The Representation of Labour in Capitalism*, edited by Diane Elson, 115–180. London: CSE Books.

Engel, Alexander. 2013. "Futures and Risk: The Rise and Demise of the Hedger-Speculator Dichotomy." *Socio-economic Review* 11 (3): 553–576.

Esposito, Elena. 1996. "Observing Interpretation: A Sociological View of Hermeneutics." *MLN* 111 (3): 593–619.

———. 2007. *Die Fiktion der wahrscheinlichen Realität*. Frankfurt am Main: Suhrkamp.

———. 2008a. "Social Forgetting: A Systems-Theory Approach." In *Media and Cultural Memory/Medien und kulturelle Erinnerung*, edited by Astrid Erll and Ansgar Nünning, 181–190. Berlin: Walter de Gruyter.

———. 2011. *The Future of Futures: The Time of Money in Financing and Society*. Cheltenham: Edward Elgar.

———. 2013. "The Structures of Uncertainty: Performativity and Unpredictability in Economic Operations." *Economy and Society* 42 (1): 102–129.

Esposito, Roberto. 2008. *Bios: Biopolitics and Philosophy*. Minneapolis: University of Minnesota Press.

Ewald, François. 1986. *Der Vorsorgestaat*. Frankfurt am Main: Suhrkamp.

———. 2002. "The Return of Descartes's Malicious Demon: An Outline of a Philosophy of Precaution." In *Embracing Risk: The Changing Culture of Insurance and Responsibility*, edited by Tom Baker and Jonathan Simon, 273–301. Chicago: University of Chicago Press.

Farias, Ignacio. 2014. "Virtual Attractors, Actual Assemblages: How Luhmann's Theory of Communication Complements Actor-Network Theory." *European Journal of Social Theory* 17 (1): 24–41.

Feher, Michel. 2009. "Self-Appreciation; or, the Aspirations of Human Capital." *Public Culture* 21 (1): 21–41.

Ferguson, Thomas, and Robert Johnson. 2010. "Too Big to Bail: The 'Paulson Put,' US Presidential Politics, and the Global Financial Meltdown." In *The Great Credit Crash*, edited by Martijn Konings, 119–169. London: Verso.

Foster, John. 2005. "From Simplistic to Complex Systems in Economics." *Cambridge Journal of Economics* 29 (6): 873–892.

Foster, John Bellamy, and Fred Magdoff. 2009. *The Great Financial Crisis: Causes and Consequences*. New York: Monthly Review Press.

Foucault, Michel. 1978–86. *The History of Sexuality*, 3 vols. New York: Vintage Books.

————. 2003 [1976]. *"Society Must Be Defended."* New York: Palgrave Macmillan.

————. 2007 [1978]. *Security, Territory, Population.* New York: Palgrave Macmillan.

————. 2008 [1979]. *The Birth of Biopolitics.* New York: Palgrave Macmillan.

Fraser, Nancy. 2013. "A Triple Movement? Parsing the Politics of Crisis after Polanyi." *New Left Review* 81 (May–June): 119–132.

Freixas, Xavier. 2009. "Monetary Policy in a Systemic Crisis." *Oxford Review of Economic Policy* 25 (4): 630–653.

Friedman, Milton. 1956. "The Quantity Theory of Money: A Restatement." In *Studies in the Quantity Theory of Money,* edited by Milton Friedman, 3–21. Chicago: University of Chicago Press.

————. 1982. "Monetary Policy: Theory and Practice." *Journal of Money, Credit and Banking* 14 (1): 98–118.

Fullwiler, Scott T. 2003. "Timeliness and the Fed's Daily Tactics." *Journal of Economic Issues* 37 (4): 851–880.

Gai, Prasanna, Andrew Haldane, and Sujit Kapadia. 2011. "Complexity, Concentration and Contagion." *Journal of Monetary Economics* 58 (5): 453–470.

Gaines, T. C. 1962. *Techniques of Treasury Debt Management.* New York: Free Press of Glencoe.

Gamble, Andrew. 1996. *Hayek: The Iron Cage of Liberty.* Cambridge: Polity.

————. 2009. *The Spectre at the Feast: Capitalist Crisis and the Politics of Recession.* New York: Palgrave Macmillan.

————. 2014. *Crisis without End? The Unravelling of Western Prosperity.* New York: Palgrave Macmillan.

Gane, Nicholas. 2014. "The Emergence of Neoliberalism: Thinking through and beyond Michel Foucault's Lectures on Biopolitics." *Theory, Culture and Society* 31 (4): 3–27.

————. 2015. "Central Banking, Technocratic Governance and the Financial Crisis: Placing Quantitative Easing into Question." *Sociologia* 4: 381–396.

Goebel, Thomas. 1997. "The Political Economy of American Populism from Jackson to the New Deal." *Studies in American Political Development* 11 (1): 109–148.

Goede, Marieke de. 2008. "The Politics of Preemption and the War on Terror in Europe." *European Journal of International Relations* 14 (1): 161–185.

————. 2012. *Speculative Security: The Politics of Pursuing Terrorist Monies.* Minneapolis: University of Minnesota Press.

Goldbach, Roman. 2015. "Asymmetric Influence in Global Banking Regulation: Transnational Harmonization, the Competition State, and the Roots of Regulatory Failure." *Review of International Political Economy* 22 (6): 1087–1127.

Golub, Stephen, Ayse Kaya, and Michael Reay. 2015. "What Were They Thinking? The Federal Reserve in the Run-Up to the 2008 Financial Crisis." *Review of International Political Economy* 22 (4): 657–692.

Goodhart, Charles. 1999. "Myths about the Lender of Last Resort." *International Finance* 2 (3): 339–360.

———. 2001. "What Weight Should Be Given to Asset Prices in the Measurement of Inflation?" *Economic Journal* 111 (June): F335–F356.

———. 2011. "The Macro-prudential Authority: Powers, Scope and Accountability." *OECD Journal: Financial Market Trends* (2): 97–120.

Goodspeed, Tyler Beck. 2012. *Rethinking the Keynesian Revolution: Keynes, Hayek, and the Wicksell Connection.* Oxford: Oxford University Press.

Gorton, Gary. 2012. *Misunderstanding Financial Crises. Why We Don't See Them Coming.* Oxford: Oxford University Press.

Gorton, Gary, and Andrew Metrick. 2012. "Securitized Banking and the Run on Repo." *Journal of Financial Economics* 104: 425–451.

Graeber, David. 2011. "Value, Politics and Democracy in the United States." *Current Sociology* 59 (2): 186–199.

Granovetter, Mark, and Richard Swedberg, eds. 2011. *The Sociology of Economic Life.* Boulder: Westview Press.

Greider, William. 1987. *Secrets of the Temple: How the Federal Reserve Runs the Country.* New York: Simon & Schuster.

Habermas, Jürgen. 1981. *Theory of Communicative Action.* Boston: Beacon Press.

Habermas, Jürgen, and Niklas Luhmann. 1971. *Theorie der Gesellschaft oder Sozialtechnologie.* Frankfurt am Main: Suhrkamp.

Haldane, Andrew G., and Robert M. May. 2011. "Systemic Risk in Banking Ecosystems." *Nature* 469: 351–355.

Hamowy, Ronald. 1987. *The Scottish Enlightenment and the Theory of Spontaneous Order.* Carbondale: Southern Illinois University Press.

Hardt, Michael, and Antonio Negri. 2001. *Empire.* Cambridge: Harvard University Press.

Hawtrey, R. G. 1919. *Currency and Credit.* London: Longmans, Green and Co.

———. 1922. "The Federal Reserve System of the United States." *Journal of the Royal Statistical Society* 85 (2): 224–269.

———. 1932. *The Art of Central Banking.* London: Longmans, Green and Co.

Hay, Colin. 2016. "Good in a Crisis: The Ontological Institutionalism of Social Constructivism." *New Political Economy* 21 (6): 520–535.

Hayek, Friedrich. 1933. *Monetary Theory and the Trade Cycle.* New York: Sentry Press.

———. 1937. "Economics and Knowledge." *Economica* 4 (13): 33–54.

———. 1949. *Individualism and Economic Order.* London: Routledge & Kegan Paul.

———. 1952. *The Sensory Order. An Inquiry into the Foundations of Theoretical Psychology.* Chicago: University of Chicago Press.

———. 1960. *The Constitution of Liberty.* Chicago: University of Chicago Press.

———. 1965 [1939]. "Introduction." In Henry Thornton, *An Enquiry into the Nature and Effects of the Paper Credit of Great Britain*, 11–63. New York: Augustus M. Kelley.

———. 1967. *Studies in Philosophy, Politics and Economics*. London: Routledge & Kegan Paul.

———. 1973. *Law, Legislation and Liberty. Vol. 1: Rules and Order*. London: Routledge.

———. 1973–79. *Law, Legislation and Liberty*. 3 vols. Chicago: University of Chicago Press.

———. 1976a. *Denationalisation of Money*. London: Institute of Economic Affairs.

———. 1976b. *Law, Legislation and Liberty. Vol. 2: The Mirage of Social Justice*. Chicago: University of Chicago Press.

———. 1979. "Toward a Free Market Monetary System." *Journal of Libertarian Studies* 3 (1): 1–8.

———. 1988. *The Fatal Conceit: The Errors of Socialism*. London: Routledge.

Helleiner, Eric. 2010. "What Role for the New Financial Stability Board? The Politics of International Standards after the Crisis." *Global Policy* 1 (3): 282–290.

———. 2014. *The Status Quo Crisis: Global Financial Governance after the 2008 Meltdown*. Ithaca: Cornell University Press.

Hetzel, Robert L. 1991. "Too Big to Fail: Origins, Consequences, and Outlook." *Federal Reserve Bank of Richmond Economic Review* 77 (November/December): 3–15.

Hogan, Thomas L., Linh Le, and Alexander William Salter. 2015. "Ben Bernanke and Bagehot's Rules." *Journal of Money, Credit and Banking* 47 (2–3): 333–348.

Hohn, Hans-Willy. 1984. *Die Zerstörung der Zeit: Wie aus einem göttlichen Gut eine Handelsware wurde*. Frankfurt am Main: Fischer Taschenbuch.

Holmes, Douglas R. 2013. *Economy of Words: Communicative Imperatives in Central Banks*. Chicago: University of Chicago Press.

Honig, Bonnie. 2009. *Emergency Politics: Paradox, Law, Democracy*. Princeton: Princeton University Press.

Honneth, Axel. 2014. *Freedom's Right: The Social Foundations of Democratic Life*. New York: Columbia University Press.

Horwitz, Steven. 2001. "From Smith to Menger to Hayek: Liberalism in the Spontaneous-Order Tradition." *Independent Review* 6 (1): 81–97.

Hudson, Michael. 2012. *The Bubble and Beyond: Fictitious Capital, Debt Deflation and Global Crisis*. New York: ISLET.

———. 2015. *Killing the Host: How Financial Parasites and Debt Bondage Destroy the Global Economy*. Petrolia: CounterPunch.

Human, Oliver. 2015. "Potential Novelty: Towards an Understanding of Novelty without an Event." *Theory, Culture and Society* 32 (4): 45–63.

Hume, David. 1985 [1752]. "Of Money." In *Essays: Moral, Political, and Literary,* edited by Eugene F. Miller, 281–294. Indianapolis: Liberty Fund.

Hüser, Anne-Caroline. 2015. "Too Interconnected to Fail: A Survey of the Interbank Networks Literature." SAFE Working Paper Series no. 91, www.econstor.eu/bitstream/10419/107770/1/820295841.pdf.

Huysmans, Jef. 2008. "The Jargon of Exception: Schmitt, Agamben and the Absence of Political Society." *International Political Sociology* 2 (2): 165–183.

Hyman, Louis. 2011. *Debtor Nation: The History of America in Red Ink.* Princeton: Princeton University Press.

Ingham, Geoffrey. 2004. *The Nature of Money.* Cambridge: Polity.

Issing, Otmar. 2009. "Asset Prices and Monetary Policy." *Cato Journal* 29 (1): 45–51.

Johns, Fleur. 2005. "Guantánamo Bay and the Annihilation of the Exception." *European Journal of International Law* 16 (4): 613–635.

Jones, Kenneth, and Barry Kolatch. 1999. "The Federal Safety Net, Banking Subsidies, and Implications for Financial Modernization." *FDIC Banking Review* 12 (1): 1–17.

Joseph, Jonathan. 2013. "Resilience as Embedded Neoliberalism: A Governmentality Approach." *Resilience: International Policies, Practices and Discourses* 1 (1): 38–52.

Jurdjevic, Mark. 2001. "Virtue, Commerce, and the Enduring Florentine Republican Moment: Reintegrating Italy into the Atlantic Republican Debate." *Journal of the History of Ideas* 62 (4): 721–743.

Kalyvas, Andreas, and Ira Katznelson. 2008. *Liberal Beginnings: Making a Republic for the Moderns.* Cambridge: Cambridge University Press.

Kane, Edward J. 1975. "New Congressional Restraints and Federal Reserve Independence." *Challenge* 18 (5): 37–44.

———. 2013. "Gaps and Wishful Thinking in the Theory and Practice of Central-Bank Policymaking." In *States, Banks and the Financing of the Economy: Monetary Policy and Regulatory Perspectives,* edited by Morten Balling, Ernest Gnan, and Patricia Jackson, 135–158. Vienna: SUERF.

Kaplan, Michael. 2003. "Iconomics: The Rhetoric of Speculation." *Public Culture* 15 (3): 477–493.

Kazin, Michael. 1998. *The Populist Persuasion: An American History.* Ithaca: Cornell University Press.

Keen, Steve. 2011. *Debunking Economics: The Naked Emperor Dethroned?* London: Zed Books.

———. 2017. *Can We Avoid Another Financial Crisis?* Cambridge: Polity.

Kessler, Oliver. 2009. "Towards an Economic Sociology of the Subprime Crisis?" *economic sociology_the european electronic newsletter* 10 (2): 11–16.

———. 2013. "Sleeping with the Enemy? On Hayek, Constructivist Thought, and the Current Economic Crisis." *Review of International Studies* 38 (2): 275–299.

Kiersey, Nicholas. 2011. "Everyday Neoliberalism and the Subjectivity of Crisis: Post-political Control in an Era of Financial Turmoil." *Journal of Critical Globalisation Studies* 4: 23–44.

———. 2017. *Negotiating Crisis: Neoliberal Power in Austerity Ireland.* London: Rowman & Littlefield International.

Kirshner, Jonathan. 1999. "Inflation: Paper Dragon or Trojan Horse?" *Review of International Political Economy* 6 (4): 609–618.

Knafo, Samuel. 2007. "Political Marxism and Value Theory: Bridging the Gap between Theory and History." *Historical Materialism* 15 (2): 75–104.

———. 2013. *The Making of Modern Finance: Liberal Governance and the Gold Standard.* New York: Routledge.

Knodt, Eva M. 1995. "Foreword." In Niklas Luhmann, *Social Systems*, ix–xxxvi. Stanford: Stanford University Press.

Kohn, Meir. 1999. "Early Deposit Banking." Working Paper 99-03, Department of Economics, Dartmouth College.

Kolb, Robert W. 2011. *The Financial Crisis of Our Time.* Oxford: Oxford University Press.

Konings, Martijn. 2010. "The Pragmatic Sources of Modern Power." *European Journal of Sociology* 51 (1): 55–91.

———. 2011. *The Development of American Finance.* New York: Cambridge University Press.

———. 2012. "Imagined Double Movements: Progressive Thought and the Specter of Neoliberal Populism." *Globalizations* 9 (4): 609–622.

———. 2015. *The Emotional Logic of Capitalism: What Progressives Have Missed.* Stanford: Stanford University Press.

Koselleck, Reinhart. 1981. "Modernity and the Planes of Historicity." *Economy and Society* 10 (2): 166–183.

———. 2002. *The Practice of Conceptual History: Timing History, Spacing Concepts.* Stanford: Stanford University Press.

———. 2006. "Crisis." *Journal of the History of Ideas* 67 (2): 357–400.

Kotz, David. M. 2015. *The Rise and Fall of Neoliberal Capitalism.* Cambridge: Harvard University Press.

Krugman, Paul. 2009. *The Conscience of a Liberal.* New York: Norton.

Laidler, David. 1981. "Monetarism: An Interpretation and an Assessment." *Economic Journal* 91 (March): 1–28.

———. 2004a. "From Bimetallism to Monetarism: The Shifting Political Affiliation of the Quantity Theory." In *Political Events and Economic Ideas*, edited by Ingo Barens, Volker Caspari, and Bertram Schefold. Cheltenham: Edward Elgar.

———. 2004b. "Central Banks as Lenders of Last Resort: Trendy or Passé?" EPRI Working Paper Series no. 2004–8.

Lange, Oskar. 1970 [1939]. "On the Economic Theory of Socialism." In *On the Economic Theory of Socialism*, edited by B. E. Lippincott, 57–142. New York: August M. Kelley Publishers.

Langley, Paul. 2008. *The Everyday Life of Global Finance: Saving and Borrowing in Anglo-America*. Oxford: Oxford University Press.

———. 2013a. "Anticipating Uncertainty, Reviving Risk? On the Stress Testing of Finance in Crisis." *Economy and Society* 42 (1): 51–73.

———. 2013b. "Toxic Assets, Turbulence and Biopolitical Security: Governing the Crisis of Global Financial Circulation." *Security Dialogue* 44 (2): 111–126.

Lapavitsas, Costas. 2014. *Profiting without Producing: How Finance Exploits Us All*. London: Verso.

Latour, Bruno. 1988. *The Pasteurization of France*. Cambridge: Harvard University Press.

———. 1999. *Pandora's Hope: Essays on the Reality of Science Studies*. Cambridge: Harvard University Press.

———. 2004. "Why Has Critique Run out of Steam? From Matters of Fact to Matters of Concern." *Critical Inquiry* 30 (2): 225–248.

———. 2013. *An Inquiry into Modes of Existence: An Anthropology of the Moderns*. Cambridge: Harvard University Press.

———. 2014. "On Some of the Affects of Capitalism." Lecture given at the Royal Academy, Copenhagen, February 26.

Law, John. 1992. "Notes on the Theory of the Actor-Network: Ordering, Strategy and Heterogeneity." *Systems Practice* 5 (4): 379–393.

———. 2009. "Actor Network Theory and Material Semiotics." In *The New Blackwell Companion to Social Theory*, edited by Bryan S. Turner, 141–158. Oxford: Wiley.

Lazzarato, Maurizio. 2009. "Neoliberalism in Action: Inequality, Insecurity and the Reconstitution of the Social." *Theory, Culture and Society* 26 (6): 109–133.

———. 2012. *The Making of the Indebted Man*. South Pasadena: Semiotext(e).

———. 2015. *Governing by Debt*. South Pasadena: Semiotext(e).

Le Goff, Jacques. 1998. *Your Money or Your Life*. New York: Zone Books.

Lears, Jackson. 2003. *Something for Nothing: Luck in America*. New York: Penguin.

Lee, Benjamin, and Randy Martin, eds. 2016. *Derivatives and the Wealth of Societies*. Chicago: University of Chicago Press.

Lemke, Thomas. 2007. "An Indigestible Meal? Foucault, Governmentality and State Theory." *Distinktion* 8 (2): 43–64.

Levitin, Adam J. 2011. "In Defense of Bailouts." *Georgetown Law Journal* 99 (2): 435–514.

Levy, Jonathan. 2014. "Accounting for Profit and the History of Capital." *Critical Historical Studies* 1 (2): 171–214.

Levy-Carciente, Sary, Dror Y. Kenett, Adam Avakian, H. Eugene Stanley, and Shlomo Havlin. 2015. "Dynamical Macroprudential Stress Testing Using Network Theory." *Journal of Banking and Finance* (59): 164–181.

Leyshon, Andrew, and Nigel Thrift. 2007. "The Capitalization of Almost Everything: The Future of Finance and Capitalism." *Theory, Culture and Society* 24 (7–8): 97–115.

Long, J. Bradford De. 2000. "The Triumph of Monetarism?" *Journal of Economic Perspectives* 14 (1): 83–94.

Lorey, Isabel. 2015. *State of Insecurity: Government of the Precarious*. London: Verso.

Lucas, Robert. 1972. "Expectations and the Neutrality of Money." *Journal of Economic Theory* 4 (2): 103–124.

———. 1976. "Econometric Policy Evaluation: A Critique." *Carnegie-Rochester Conference Series* 1: 19–46.

Luhmann, Niklas. 1976. "The Future Cannot Begin: Temporal Structures in Modern Society." *Social Research* 43 (1): 130–152.

———. 1978. "Temporalization of Complexity." In *Sociocybernetics: An Actor-Oriented Social System Approach*, vol. 2, edited by R. F. Geyer and J. van der Zouwen, 95–111. Leiden: Martinus Nijhoff Social Sciences Division.

———. 1988. *Die Wirtschaft der Gesellschaft*. Frankfurt am Main: Suhrkamp.

———. 1995. *Social Systems*. Stanford: Stanford University Press.

———. 1998. *Observations on Modernity*. Stanford: Stanford University Press.

———. 2002a. *Risk: A Sociological Theory*. New Brunswick: Transaction.

———. 2002b. *Theories of Distinction: Redescribing the Descriptions of Modernity*. Stanford: Stanford University Press.

———. 2013. *Introduction to Systems Theory*. Cambridge: Polity.

MacGilvray, Eric. 2011. *The Invention of Market Freedom*. Cambridge: Cambridge University Press.

Mackenzie, Donald. 2006. *An Engine, Not a Camera: How Financial Models Shape Markets*. Cambridge: MIT Press.

Malabou, Catherine. 2000. "The Future of Hegel: Plasticity, Temporality, Dialectic." *Hypatia* 15 (4): 196–220.

————. 2008. *What Should We Do with Our Brain?* New York: Fordham University Press.

Malysheva, Nadezhda, and John R. Walter. 2010. "How Large Has the Federal Financial Safety Net Become?" *Federal Reserve Bank of Richmond Economic Quarterly* 96 (3): 273–290.

Marazzi, Christian. 2007. "Rules for the Incommensurable." *SubStance* 36 (1): 11–36.

Martin, Randy. 2002. *Financialization of Daily Life*. Philadelphia: Temple University Press.

————. 2015. *Knowledge Ltd: Toward a Social Logic of the Derivative*. Philadelphia: Temple University Press.

Marx, Karl. 1990 [1867]. *Capital*, vol. 1. London: Penguin.

Massumi, Brian. 2005. "The Future Birth of the Affective Fact." *Conference Proceedings: Genealogies of Biopolitics*: 1–12.

————. 2007. "Potential Politics and the Primacy of Preemption." *Theory and Event* 10 (2).

————. 2014. *The Power at the End of the Economy*. Durham: Duke University Press.

Maturana, Humberto, and Francisco Varela. 1992. *The Tree of Knowledge: The Biological Roots of Human Understanding*. Boston: Shambhala.

Maux, Laurent Le, and Laurence Scialom. 2013. "Central Banks and Financial Stability: Rediscovering the Lender-of-Last-Resort Practice in a Finance Economy." *Cambridge Journal of Economics* 37 (1): 1–16.

Mayer, Martin. 1974. *The Bankers*. New York: Weybright and Talley.

Mayer, Thomas. 1999. *Monetary Policy and the Great Inflation in the United States: The Federal Reserve and the Failure of Macroeconomic Policy, 1965–79*. Cheltenham: Edward Elgar.

McCarty, Nolan. 2013. "Complexity, Capacity, and Capture." In *Preventing Regulatory Capture: Special Interest Influence and How to Limit It*, edited by Daniel Carpenter and David A. Moss, 99–123. Cambridge: Cambridge University Press.

McCloud, Laura, and Rachel E. Dwyer. 2011. "The Fragile American: Hardship and Financial Troubles in the 21st Century." *Sociological Quarterly* 52 (1): 13–35.

Mehrling, Perry. 1999. "The Vision of Hyman P. Minsky." *Journal of Economic Behavior and Organization* 39 (2): 129–158.

————. 2000a. "Minsky and Modern Finance: The Case of Long Term Capital Management." *Journal of Portfolio Management* 26 (Winter): 81–88.

————. 2000b. "The State as Financial Intermediary." *Journal of Economic Issues* 34 (2): 365–368.

————. 2011. *The New Lombard Street: How the Fed Became the Dealer of Last Resort*. Princeton: Princeton University Press.

————. 2012. "Three Principles for Market-Based Credit Regulation." *American Economic Review* 102 (3): 107–112.

————. 2015. s.v. "Minsky, Hyman (1919–1996)." In *The New Palgrave Dictionary of Economics*, online ed., edited by Steven N. Durlauf and Lawrence E. Blume. Palgrave Macmillan.

Meikle, Scott. 1994. "Aristotle on Money." *Phronesis* 39 (1): 26–44.

Melzer, Thomas C. 1986. "Are There Risks to Regulating Bank Risks?" Remarks to the St. Louis Chapter of the Robert Morris Associates (March 11), https://fraser.stlouisfed.org/files/docs/historical/frbsl_history/presidents/melzer/melzer_19860311.pdf.

————. 1995. "The Evolving U.S. Payments System: A Central Banker's Viewpoint." Remarks to the National Payments System Bank Administration Institute Foundations, Washington, DC (October 16), https://fraser.stlouisfed.org/scribd/?item_id=18788&filepath=/files/docs/historical/frbsl_history/presidents/melzer/melzer_19951016.pdf.

Miller, Peter, and Nikolas Rose. 2008. *Governing the Present: Administering Economic, Social and Personal Life*. Cambridge: Polity.

Minsky, Hyman P. 1957. "Central Banking and Money Market Changes." *Quarterly Journal of Economics* 71 (2): 171–187.

————. 1977. "The Financial Instability Hypothesis: An Interpretation of Keynes and an Alternative to 'Standard' Theory." *Challenge* (March–April): 20–27.

————. 1980. "Capitalist Financial Processes and the Instability of Capitalism." *Journal of Economic Issues* 14 (2): 505–523.

————. 1982. *Can "It" Happen Again?* New York: Sharpe.

————. 1986. "The Evolution of Financial Institutions and the Performance of the Economy." *Journal of Economic Issues* 20 (2): 345–353.

————. 1996. "Uncertainty and the Institutional Structure of Capitalist Economies: Remarks upon Receiving the Veblen-Commons Award." *Journal of Economic Issues* 30 (2): 357–368.

————. 2008 [1975]. *John Maynard Keynes*. New York: McGraw-Hill.

————. 2008 [1986]. *Stabilizing an Unstable Economy*. New York: McGraw Hill.

Mints, Lloyd W. 1945. *A History of Banking Theory in Great Britain and the United States*. Chicago: University of Chicago Press.

Mirowski, Philip. 2013. *Never Let a Serious Crisis Go to Waste: How Neoliberalism Survived the Financial Meltdown*. London: Verso.

Mises, Ludwig von. 1935. "Economic Calculation in the Socialist Commonwealth." In *Collectivist Economic Planning*, edited by Friedrich Hayek, 87–130. London: Routledge & Kegan Paul.

Mishkin, Frederic S. 2006. "How Big a Problem Is Too Big to Fail? A Review of Gary Stern and Ron Feldman's *Too Big to Fail: The Hazards of Bank Bailouts.*" *Journal of Economic Literature* 44 (December): 988–1004.

Mitropoulos, Angela. 2012. *Contract and Contagion: From Biopolitics to Oikonomia.* Minor Compositions.

Moeller, Hans-Georg. 2006. *Luhmann Explained: From Souls to Systems.* Chicago: Open Court.

———. 2012. *The Radical Luhmann.* New York: Columbia University Press.

Morgan, E. Victor. 1943. *The Theory and Practice of Central Banking.* Cambridge: Cambridge University Press.

Muhle, Maria. 2014. "A Genealogy of Biopolitics: The Notion of Life in Canguilhem and Foucault." In *The Government of Life: Foucault, Biopolitics, and Neoliberalism,* edited by Vanessa Lemm and Miguel Vatter, 77–97. New York: Fordham University Press.

Muniesa, Fabian. 2011. "A Flank Movement in the Understanding of Valuation." *Sociological Review* 59 (s2): 24–38.

Negri, Antonio. 1999. "Value and Affect." *boundary 2* 26 (2): 77–88.

Neocleous, Mark. 2008. *Critique of Security.* Edinburgh: Edinburgh University Press.

Nesvetailova, Anastasia. 2014. "'Liquidity' in Light of the Shadow Banking System: Lessons from the Two Crises." In *Economic Policy and the Financial Crisis,* edited by Łukasz Mamica and Pasquale Tridico, 132–147. Abingdon: Routledge.

———. 2015. "A Crisis of the Overcrowded Future: Shadow Banking and the Political Economy of Financial Innovation." *New Political Economy* 20 (3): 431–453.

Nitzan, Jonathan, and Shimshon Bichler. 2009. *Capital as Power. A Study of Order and Creorder.* Abingdon: Routledge.

Ong, Aihwa. 2006. *Neoliberalism as Exception: Mutations in Citizenship and Sovereignty.* Durham: Duke University Press.

Opitz, Sven, and Ute Tellmann. 2015. "Future Emergencies: Temporal Politics in Law and Economy." *Theory, Culture and Society* 32 (2): 107–129.

Orléan, Andre. 1989. "Mimetic Contagion and Speculative Bubbles." *Theory and Decision* 27 (1–2): 63–92.

Palan, Ronen. 2000. "A World of Their Making: An Evaluation of the Constructivist Critique in International Relations." *Review of International Studies* 26 (4): 575–598.

———. 2013. "The Financial Crisis and Intangible Value." *Capital and Class* 37 (1): 65–77.

———. 2015. "Futurity, Pro-cyclicality and Financial Crises." *New Political Economy* 20 (3): 367–385.

Palley, Thomas I. 2013. *Financialization: The Economics of Finance Capital Domi-nation*. New York: Palgrave Macmillan.

Pangle, Thomas L. 1988. *The Spirit of Modern Republicanism: The Moral Vision of the American Founders and the Philosophy of Locke*. Chicago: University of Chicago Press.

Panitch, Leo, and Sam Gindin. 2012. *The Making of Global Capitalism: The Po-litical Economy of American Empire*. London: Verso.

Papaioannou, Theo. 2012. *Reading Hayek in the 21st Century: A Critical Inquiry into His Political Thought*. New York: Palgrave Macmillan.

Parsons, Talcott. 1951. *The Social System*. New York: Free Press.

Peck, Jamie. 2010. *Constructions of Neoliberal Reason*. Oxford: Oxford University Press.

Petsoulas, Christina. 2001. *Hayek's Liberalism and Its Origins: His Idea of Sponta-neous Order and the Scottish Enlightenment*. Abingdon: Routledge.

Pocock, J. G. A. 1975. *The Machiavellian Moment: Florentine Political Thought and the Atlantic Republican Tradition*. Princeton: Princeton University Press.

Polanyi, Karl. 1944. *The Great Transformation*. New York: Farrar & Rinehart.

Posen, Adam S. 2006. "Why Central Banks Should Not Burst Bubbles." *Inter-national Finance* 9 (1): 109–124.

Postel, Charles. 2009. *The Populist Vision*. Oxford: Oxford University Press.

Rasch, William. 2002. "Introduction: The Self-Positing Society." In Niklas Luhmann, *Theories of Distinction: Redescribing the Descriptions of Modernity*, 1–30. Stanford: Stanford University Press.

Ricks, Morgan. 2016. *The Money Problem: Rethinking Financial Regulation*. Chi-cago: University of Chicago Press.

Ritter, Gretchen. 1999. *Goldbugs and Greenbacks: The Antimonopoly Tradition and the Politics of Finance in America, 1865–1896*. Cambridge: Cambridge Uni-versity Press.

Rixen, Thomas. 2013. "Offshore Financial Centres, Shadow Banking and Juris-dictional Competition: Incrementalism and Feeble Re-regulation." In *Great Expectations, Slow Transformations: Incremental Change in Post-crisis Regula-tion*, edited by Manuela Moschella and Eleni Tsingou, 95–124. Colchester: ECPR Press.

Rotman, Brian. 1987. *Signifying Nothing: The Semiotics of Zero*. London: Mac-millan.

Roubini, Nouriel. 2006. "Why Central Banks Should Burst Bubbles." *Interna-tional Finance* 9 (1): 87–107.

Rubin, Isaak. 1972. *Essays on Marx's Theory of Value*. Detroit: Black & Red.

Rude, Christopher. 2010. "The World Economic Crisis and the Federal Re-serve's Response to It: August 2007–December 2008." *Studies in Political Economy* (85): 125–148.

Santner, Eric L. 2011. *The Royal Remains: The People's Two Bodies and the End-games of Sovereignty*. Chicago: University of Chicago Press.

Sargent, Thomas J. 1982. "The Ends of Four Big Inflations." In *Inflation: Causes and Effects*, edited by Robert E. Hall, 41–98. Chicago: University of Chicago Press.

Schäfer, Armin, and Wolfgang Streeck, eds. 2013. *Politics in the Age of Austerity*. Cambridge: Polity.

Scheuerman, William E. 1997. "The Unholy Alliance of Carl Schmitt and Friedrich A. Hayek." *Constellations* 4 (2): 172–188.

Schui, Florian. 2014. *Austerity: The Great Failure*. New Haven: Yale University Press.

Schwartz, Anna J. 1987. "The Lender of Last Resort and the Federal Safety Net." *Journal of Financial Services Research* 1 (1): 1–17.

Seabrooke, Leonard. 2007. "Varieties of Economic Constructivism in Political Economy: Uncertain Times Call for Disparate Measures." *Review of International Political Economy* 14 (2): 371–385.

Serres, Michel. 1982. *The Parasite*. Minneapolis: University of Minnesota Press.

Sgambati, Stefano. 2015. "Rethinking Banking: Debt Discounting and the Making of Modern Money as Liquidity." *New Political Economy* 21 (3): 274–290.

Shackle, G. L. S. 1972. *Epistemics and Economics: A Critique of Economic Doctrines*. Cambridge: Cambridge University Press.

Sheehan, Jonathan, and Dror Wahrman. 2015. *Invisible Hands: Self-Organization and the Eighteenth Century*. Chicago: University of Chicago Press.

Silber, William L. 2012. *Volcker: The Triumph of Persistence*. New York: Bloomsbury.

Simmel, Georg. 2011 [1900]. *Philosophy of Money*. New York: Routledge.

Smith, Adam. 1999 [1776]. *The Wealth of Nations*, bks. 1–3. London: Penguin.

Soederberg, Susanne. 2014. *Debtfare States and the Poverty Industry: Money, Discipline and the Surplus Population*. Abingdon: Routledge.

Sprague, Irvine H. 2000. *Bailout: An Insider's Account of Bank Failures and Rescues*. New York: Beard Books.

Stanley, Liam. 2014. " 'We're Reaping What We Sowed': Everyday Crisis Narratives and Acquiescence to the Age of Austerity." *New Political Economy* 19 (6): 895–917.

Stern, Gary H., and Ron J. Feldman. 2004. *Too Big to Fail: The Hazards of Bank Bailouts*. Washington, DC: Brookings Institution Press.

Stigler, George. 1971. "The Theory of Economic Regulation." *Bell Journal of Economics and Management Science* 2 (1): 3–21.

Stiglitz, Joseph. 2010. *Freefall: America, Free Markets, and the Sinking of the World Economy*. New York: Norton.

Streeck, Wolfgang. 2012. "How to Study Contemporary Capitalism?" *European Journal of Sociology* 53 (1): 1–28.

———. 2014. *Buying Time: The Delayed Crisis of Democratic Capitalism*. London: Verso.

Stuckler, David, and Sanjay Basu. 2013. *The Body Economic: Why Austerity Kills*. New York: Penguin.

Tabb, William K. 2012. *The Restructuring of Capitalism in Our Time*. New York: Columbia University Press.

Taylor, Mark C. 2008. *Confidence Games: Money and Markets in a World without Redemption*. Chicago: University of Chicago Press.

Tellmann, Ute. 2009. "Imagining Catastrophe: Scenario Planning and the Striving for Epistemic Security." *economic sociology_the european electronic newsletter* 10 (2): 17–21.

Tellmann, Ute, Sven Opitz, and Urs Staeheli. 2012. "Operations of the Global: Explorations of Connectivity." *Distinktion: Scandinavian Journal of Social Theory* 13 (3): 209–214.

Thompson, Grahame. 2013. "Activist Central Banking and Its Possible Consequences." Working Paper no. 80, Department of Business and Politics, Copenhagen Business School.

Thornhill, Chris. 2006. "Niklas Luhmann: A Sociological Transformation of Political Legitimacy?" *Distinktion* 7 (2): 33–53.

Thornton, Henry. 1965 [1802]. *An Enquiry into the Nature and Effects of the Paper Credit of Great Britain*. New York: Augustus M. Kelley.

Thrift, Nigel. 1990. "The Making of a Capitalist Time Consciousness." In *The Sociology of Time*, edited by John Hassard, 105–129. London: Macmillan.

Timberlake, Richard H. 1993. *Monetary Policy in the United States: An Intellectual and Institutional History*. Chicago: University of Chicago Press.

Tobin, James. 1980. *Asset Accumulation and Economic Activity: Reflections on Contemporary Macroeconomic Theory*. London: Blackwell.

Toniolo, Gianni. 2010. "What Is a Useful Central Bank? Lessons from the Interwar Years." In *What Is a Useful Central Bank?*, proceedings from Norges Bank's symposium, November 17–18, edited by Sigbjørn Atle Berg, Øyvind Eitrheim, Jan F. Qvigstad, and Marius Ryel, 51–78. Norges Bank Occasional Papers.

Tymoigne, Eric, and L. Randall Wray. 2014. *The Rise and Fall of Money Manager Capitalism: Minsky's Half Century from World War Two to the Great Recession*. Abingdon: Routledge.

Underhill, Geoffrey R. D. 2015. "The Emerging Post-crisis Financial Architecture: The Path-Dependency of Ideational Adverse Selection." *British Journal of Politics and International Relations* 17 (3): 461–493.

Vatter, Miguel. 2014. "Foucault and Hayek: Republican Law and Liberal Civil Society." In *The Government of Life: Foucault, Biopolitics, and Neoliberalism*, edited by Vanessa Lemm and Miguel Vatter, 163–184. New York: Fordham University Press.

Viner, Jacob. 1937. *Studies in the Theory of International Trade*. New York: Harper & Brothers.

Vogl, Joseph. 2014. "The Sovereignty Effect: Markets and Power in the Economic Regime." *Qui Parle* 23 (1): 125–155.

———. 2015. *The Specter of Capital*. Stanford: Stanford University Press.

Volcker, Paul A. 1978. "The Role of Monetary Targets in an Age of Inflation." *Journal of Monetary Economics* 4 (2): 329–339.

———. 1979. "The Contributions and Limitations of 'Monetary' Analysis." *Federal Reserve Bank of New York Quarterly Review*: 35–41.

———. 2000. "Interview." *Commanding Heights*, PBS, September 26, www.pbs. org/wgbh/commandingheights/shared/minitext/int_paulvolcker.html.

Weber, Max. 1978. *Economy and Society*. Berkeley: University of California Press.

Weintraub, Robert E. 1977. "Some Neglected Monetary Contributions: Congressman Wright Patman (1893–1976)." *Journal of Money, Credit and Banking* 9 (4): 517–528.

———. 1978. "Congressional Supervision of Monetary Policy." *Journal of Monetary Economics* 4 (2): 341–362.

West, Robert Craig. 1977. *Banking Reform and the Federal Reserve, 1863–1923*. Ithaca: Cornell University Press.

Wheelock, David C. 2010. "Lessons Learned? Comparing the Federal Reserve's Responses to the Crises of 1929–1933 and 2007–2009." *Federal Reserve Bank of St. Louis Review* 92 (2): 89–107.

Wicker, Elmus R. 1966. *Federal Reserve Monetary Policy 1917–1933*. New York: Random House.

Wicksell, Knut. 1962 [1898]. *Interest and Prices*. New York: Sentry Press.

Williams, Jeffrey J. 2008. "Student Debt and the Spirit of Indenture." *Dissent* 55 (4): 73–78.

Woodford, Michael. 2003. *Interest and Prices: Foundations of a Theory of Monetary Policy*. Princeton: Princeton University Press.

Wray, L. Randall. 1990. *Money and Credit in Capitalist Economies: The Endogenous Money Approach*. Aldershot: Edward Elgar.

———. 2009. "The Rise and Fall of Money Manager Capitalism: A Minskian Approach." *Cambridge Journal of Economics* 33 (4): 807–828.

Young, Nancy Beck. 2000. *Wright Patman: Populism, Liberalism and the American Dream*. Dallas: Southern Methodist University Press.

Index

debt: bad debt, 118; government, 94,
121, 123; hedge financing, 16, 79,
136–137n1, 137n4; household,
5–6, 20–21, 28, 94–95, 110, 123;
money as bank debt, 1, 77, 84;
repayment obligations, 74, 76,
104–105, 110, 139n2; student,
124–125. See also leveraging
Deleuze, Gilles, 19
disembedding. See embedding and
disembedding
double-entry bookkeeping, 73–74.
See also balance sheets
double movement, 3, 12–13, 34,
135–136n1

economic determinism, critique of,
4, 8, 32–33, 35, 61–62
economism, fallacy of, 32–33
economy: cultural, 39, 129; Fordist,
10–11, 20, 37, 110–111; Hayek
on, 105–108; imaginary of, 24, 37;
Latour on, 130–131, 140n1; modern expansion of reach of, 35, 55–
57; neutrality of, 24, 58, 84–85;
ordering mechanisms, 59–60, 61,
75–76, 101–102; political, 4, 10,
18–19, 26, 39, 110–111; precapitalist bank crises, 81; premodern,
7, 57–58, 64, 70–71, 87; sovereignty in, 62–68; temporalization
in, 7, 73–74; theology and, 54, 57,
64; village fair model, 85, 138n1.
See also contingency; market; neoclassical economics; neoliberalism;
ordering; orthodox economic
theory; self-organization
education, cost of, 124–125
embedding and disembedding: current re-embedding movement,

122; in double movement concept, 3; of financial governance,
83; Polanyi and, 36; social integration and, 35
entrepreneurs, Hayek on, 104
Esposito, Roberto, 67
Ewald, François, 20, 27
exceptionalism, 26, 65, 67, 102, 119,
128
expectations: inflation control and,
96–99, 115, 121; leveraging
and, 50–52; speculation and, 49;
temporalization and, 70, 72–74,
76; too-big-to-fail and, 112–113,
114; value and, 3

Fatal Conceit, The (Hayek), 102
Federal Reserve: bank balance
sheets and, 121; under Bernanke,
118–119, 140n1; creation of,
93–94; expectations and, 115;
government debt and, 94, 121;
under Greenspan, 113, 114–116;
inflation and, 21, 95–97, 110,
112–116, 139n1; interest rate
changes by, 90, 92, 95, 113–116,
118; lender-of-last-resort function, 91, 92, 115; under Martin,
95; monetarism and, 97–99,
109–110; mop-up strategy of,
113, 115; in neoliberalism, 28,
113–114; neutral perception
of, 88; quantitative easing by,
121–122; speculation in policy
of, 109–110; under Volcker, 28,
97–99, 100, 109–114. See also
central banking
Feher, Michel, 112
financial crises: in 1929, 94, 117;
central banking function in,

Currencies:
New Thinking for Financial Times

Melinda Cooper and Martijn Konings, Series Editors

In the wake of recent events such as the global financial crisis, the Occupy Wall Street Movement, and the rise of anti-student debt activism, the need for a more sophisticated encounter between economic theory and social and political philosophy has become pressing. The growth of new forms of money and finance, which has only accelerated since the financial crisis, is recognized as one of the defining developments of our time. But even as finance continuously breaches limits and forces adjustments, much scholarly commentary remains focused on the limits of the market and the need to establish some prior state of political stability, thus succumbing to a nostalgia that blunts its critical edge. Not content to adopt a defensive posture, books in this series move beyond well-rehearsed denunciations of out-of-control markets and seek to rethink the core institutions and categories of financialized capitalism. *Currencies* will serve as a forum for work that is situated at the intersection of economics, the humanities, and the social sciences. It will include conceptually driven historical or empirical studies, genealogies of economic ideas and institutions, and work that employs new or unexplored theoretical resources to rethink key economic categories and themes.